BRIGHT NOTES

THE PLAYS OF SOPHOCLES

Intelligent Education

Nashville, Tennessee

BRIGHT NOTES: The Plays of Sophocles
www.BrightNotes.com

No part of this publication may be used or reproduced in any manner whatsoever without written permission, except in the case of brief quotations in critical articles and reviews. For permissions, contact Influence Publishers http://www.influencepublishers.com.

ISBN: 978-1-645424-54-3 (Paperback)
ISBN: 978-1-645424-55-0 (eBook)

Published in accordance with the U.S. Copyright Office Orphan Works and Mass Digitization report of the register of copyrights, June 2015.

Originally published by Monarch Press.
William Walter, 1963
2020 Edition published by Influence Publishers.

Interior design by Lapiz Digital Services. Cover Design by Thinkpen Designs.

Printed in the United States of America.

Library of Congress Cataloging-in-Publication Data forthcoming.
Names: Intelligent Education
Title: BRIGHT NOTES: The Plays of Sophocles
Subject: STU004000 STUDY AIDS / Book Notes

CONTENTS

1) Introduction to Sophocles — 1

2) Ajax — 13

3) Antigone — 26

4) Oedipus the King — 40

5) Electra — 63

6) Trachiniae — 82

7) Philoctetes — 96

8) Oedipus at Colonus — 111

9) Critical Commentary — 126

10) Essay Questions and Answers — 131

11) Bibliography and Guide to Further Research — 147

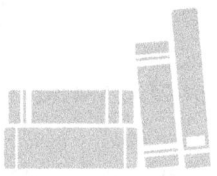

INTRODUCTION TO SOPHOCLES

THE PERSIAN WARS

546-491 B.C.: Persian rule of Greek cities in Asia Minor. Persian king: Darius. 490 B.C.: Athenian general, Miltiades, defeats Persians invading Greek mainland in battle of Marathon. 480-479 B.C.: Athens defeats Persians in naval battle of Salamis (480 B.C). Persian king: Xerxes. 479 B.C.: Remaining Persian troops defeated.

RESULTS

(1) The successful defeats of the Persians made Athens the most powerful and important city in Greece. (2) Fear of Persians led to Panhellenic unity: Delian league established with Athens in control.

GOLDEN AGE OF PERICLES (461-429 B.C.)

Pericles kept the aggressive economic policy. Athens became wealthy; the arts were encouraged and supported; Athens became the economic and cultural center of the Mediterranean world.

BRIGHT NOTES STUDY GUIDE

PELOPONNESIAN WARS (431-404 B.C.)

Rival imperialisms of Athens and Sparta caused war. 415-413 B.C.: War party of Athens sent expedition of 40,000 to conquer Sicily (ostensible purpose was to help one Sicilian city against another). Total defeat for Athens. 405 B.C.: Spartans captured and destroyed Athenian navy.

RESULTS

Athens lost all her possessions; walls of Athens torn down; pro-Spartans govern Athens.

THE TRAGIC DRAMA

Origins

Very little is known for certain about the origin of Greek drama. Aristotle says it grew out of improvisations of the dithyramb, a choral poem in honor of the god Dionysus. This early association with a religious festival was never lost, and the theater never became a commercial enterprise. An official chosen by lot selected the plays to be presented; the state supplied the actors and selected wealthy citizens to support the preparation of the choruses.

Subject Matter

The stories dramatized were usually taken from mythology. However, at least two plays on current events were written by an older contemporary of Aeschylus, Phrynichus. Aeschylus himself wrote about current events in his Persians. The use of legends from the traditional mythology did not eliminate invention, for mythological stories often had numerous versions, and, in any case, the dramatist would be obliged to focus his material, supply details of motivation, and make a series of actions relevant to his **theme**. Sometimes even well-known legends were simply changed, especially by Euripides. The kind of suspense in most of these tragedies, then, involves not so much a curiosity as to what will happen as to how it will happen. (Aristotle records that Agathon's *Anthus*, which has not survived, had both invented characters and an invented story.)

A special effect of Greek drama, frequently lost on the modern reader, is that of dramatic **irony**. This is produced when the audience knows what is going to happen to a character who speaks in ignorance of his future. A double meaning is thus frequently given to what he says, from the audience's point of view.

Perhaps the greatest qualities of tragedy attributable to the use of mythological material are seriousness and dignity. Persons and events associated with religion, known individually to the gods-some with divine parents - and with a quasi-historical character, give a kind of exalted reality to tragedy. The equivalent in the Hebrew-Christian tradition is the group of legends in the Old Testament.

The Theater

Both tragedies and comedies were presented in the open-air theater (theatron or koilon), semi-circular in shape. Tiers of seats ranged upward from the lowest level, frequently taking advantage of ground sloping to form a natural amphitheater.

Their size attests the popularity of drama: the Theater of Dionysus in Athens could seat 17,000. Performances were given twice a year in January-February for the Lenaea, or festival of the wine-press, and in March-April for the festival to Dionysus called the Greater or City Dionysia. In fifth-century Athens, until the Peloponnesian War began, the latter festival ran for six consecutive days. At the lowest level was a flat round area called the orchestra, or dancing place for the Chorus. In its center was an altar to Dionysus which was also used as a stage property in many plays. Facing the altar, in the first row center, sat the priest of Dionysus. Forming the flat end of the semi-circle was the skene, or scene building. It was a wooden or stone structure which represented the front of a house, palace, or temple, and most of the action took place on a low platform at its base (the proskenion). The three doors of the skene were used for actors' entrances as required, although most entrances, including that of the Chorus, would be made from either side, through the parodoi. The orchestra was used for the choral dances and for what action might require the actors to move forward. The top of the skene was also used for scenes set on the roof of a building. From there also descended the **deus ex machina**, the "god from the machine" used so frequently by Euripides. Since gods would be expected to descend from above, a mechanical contrivance was used to lower them to the acting area. The device, of course, is less important than the dramatic use made of it. Since the material of the plays was nearly always mythological in origin, the appearance of gods was to be expected. It will be noted in reading the plays, however, that the gods as characters are rarely performers of magic who twist the action of the mortal characters about regardless of realistic possibilities. Usually, the **deus ex machina** gives divine approval to some action which has already worked itself out in terms of character, or it may foretell the future, thus concluding the story or relating it to the dramatist's own day. (*The Rhesus* has an interesting exception.)

Another important stage device was the eccyclema, a platform which could be rolled out to reveal a tableau representing a murder which had taken place off-stage. The most frequent use of the eccyclema in tragedy is for those scenes in which the stage directions in modern translations read: "The palace doors are thrown open to reveal the bodies of. . . ." Over or near the tableau, the actor who committed the murder would then deliver his speech, usually one of justification.

In addition to being religious festivals, the dramatic presentations were contests in which first, second, and third prizes were awarded. Each tragic dramatist was required to submit a tetralogy (a group of four plays). Three were tragedies and the fourth a lighter piece. The three plays might or might not be related to one another. Although the word "trilogy" means simply a group of three, it is frequently used to describe, in Greek tragedy, three plays about the same story, or group of events. Each individual play, however, would be a separate dramatic entity. Only one trilogy has survived complete. Aeschylus' *Oresteia*.

The fourth play of a tetralogy was usually a satyr-play, deriving its name from its Chorus, which always consisted of Satyrs. These are mythological creatures, represented as men with pointed ears, short horns, and goat legs. They were attendants on Dionysus, the god of fertility and wine. Fond of riotous living and lechery, they took frank and indecent pleasure in drinking and love-making. They were usually accompanied by *Silenus*, an aged Satyr. This character of the Chorus has an obvious connection with the god in whose honor the drama festivals were held, and the plays offered a light diversion after several hours of often very serious theater. The only complete satyr-play to survive is Euripides' *Cyclops*.

All plays were presented during the day, and only very rarely, therefore, does the action call for a night scene. The actors themselves were always men, and always wore masks, perhaps so that everyone could see the dominant emotion of the character being presented. The number of speaking actors on the stage at one time did not exceed three. Any single actor would change mask and costume off-stage and re-enter as a different character. A certain larger-than-life appearance was given the actor by the use of the cothurnus, the high-soled tragic boot. Masks and costumes were apparently conventional for the character-types most frequently represented, and the audience would guess their identity immediately.

From a modern viewpoint, most aspects of the Greek theater seem confining, and, in fact, relatively little experimentation which would involve changing the physical appearance of the theater occurred. The fourth actor, though the need for him became more apparent, never appeared in tragedy; the Chorus, though its role became smaller, never disappeared. The amazing thing is the variety and dramatic effectiveness of the plays produced within the limits of the theater and its conventions.

Structure Of Tragedy

The plots of Greek tragedies cannot be reduced to a single type. Certain structural divisions of each play are, however, almost invariable:

Prologue

(prologos) This introductory section recounts background needed for understanding the action of the play. It is usually expository rather than dramatic, and indicates the starting point of subsequent action.

Parodos

The entrance of Chorus, chanting or singing. The verses usually contain further **exposition** and set the emotional tone of the play.

Episode And Stasimon

The action begins with the first **episode**, which follows the parodos. Although the number of **episodes** varies, it apparently was eventually fixed at five - the origin of the later **convention** of five acts. **Episodes** are separated by complete choral odes called stasima. The Chorus, or its leader, sometimes speaks during an **episode**, and a character sometimes speaks during, or is part of, a stasimon.

Exodos

The section after the last stasimon. It contains the final action of the play-usually not the "reversal" or **climax** - and a choral comment. Two features frequently appearing in the exodos are the messenger speech (which may also occur earlier in the play) and the deus ex machina.

Chorus

There is always a Chorus in Greek tragedy; indeed, tragedy itself originated with choral songs to which actors were added. Almost constantly present, the Chorus fulfills a number of functions. They sing and dance. They have been called the ideal audience, reacting to the action as the poet would most desire. In fact, many people who had at one time or another performed in the Chorus were probably in the audience-accounting for some of the theatrical sophistication of Athenian audiences.

By their responses to the action, the Chorus modulated the atmosphere and tone. Usually representing what might be called "typical Athenian citizens," their reactions tended to be conservative, but not submissive. They were often involved in the action's outcome. Plays were very often named for the Chorus, which is sometimes the **protagonist** (Aeschylus, Suppliants), or sometimes of particular importance (Euripides, Bacchae). Often, when the action centers on more than one character, the play may be designated by the Chorus (Sophocles, *Trachiniae*). A frequent function of the Chorus or of its leader (coryphaeus) was to question new characters coming on stage as to their identity and purpose. Since the stage had no curtain and the plays no act divisions, the choral odes were also used to represent the passage of time-a flexible interval extending from a few minutes to several days or weeks.

Although the major divisions of the plays are not indicated in most English translations, the choral odes are set apart. The Chorus was usually divided into two groups: giving a symmetrical visual effect on stage. The first lyric they sing is called the strophe ("movement"), and the second, metrically equivalent, the antistrophe ("counter-movement"). The afterpiece, marking the end of a stasimon, is called the epode. A lyric exchange of lamentation between the Chorus and an actor is called a kommos.

As tragedy developed, the role of the Chorus lessened. In Aeschylus' *Suppliants* half the play is choral; in many by Euripides and Sophocles, less than a quarter. In late tragedy the constant presence of the Chorus became an obvious hindrance to the poet, and the day of its disappearance was not far off.

SOPHOCLES' LIFE

Sophocles was born in Colonus, a part of Athens, about 495 B.C. He died about 406 B.C., his life having spanned nearly the whole of the fifth century in Athens. He lived in a time and place which saw an astonishing flowering of human genius, and to which he made a great contribution.

Sophocles won his first dramatic victory (over Aeschylus) in 468 B.C. Of the one hundred and twenty plays he probably wrote, twenty-four won first prizes, a record unequalled by any known Greek dramatist. So enthusiastic were the Athenians about his plays that he was elected one of their generals - the highest elective office in Athens. He was apparently unconcerned with practical politics, but did take an active part in the community's religious life, holding priesthoods in several cults and receiving various religious honors.

Unlike Euripides, who was said to withdraw to a cave on the island of Salamis to write his tragedies, Sophocles was famous for his sociability. Opposite attitudes prevail in the plays of each man, Euripides writing with intense concern about current events, and Sophocles writing with detachment. Sophocles disliked many of the ideas of Euripides, but he frequently borrowed technical features of Euripides' plays, and is said to have worn mourning for Euripides' death. Sophocles' son, Iophon, also wrote tragedies. Seven plays were chosen by a Byzantine anthologist as representative of Sophocles' work, as in the case of Aeschylus, and only these seven have survived.

DRAMATIC FORMS AND THEMES

Comments Of An Ancient Biographer

An ancient biographer of Sophocles made the following points about him and his plays:

1. Learned to write tragedies from Aeschylus but made innovations.

2. Didn't act in his own plays as was traditional (disputed by later critics).

3. Increased the number of choral members from 12 to 15.

4. Introduced new kinds of costumes.

5. Wrote with actors' problems and desires in mind.

6. Introduced painted scenery (Aristotle).

Dramatic Form

1. Abandonment of trilogy; plays are self-contained units.

2. Preference for dialogue over lengthy monologues; **exposition** of the past usually distributed throughout the play.

3. Preference for dramatic action over action occurring of-stage and reported by a messenger.

4. Role of Chorus reduced. Euripides also reduced portion of play given to Chorus but tended to use Chorus for lyric interludes. Sophocles usually integrates Chorus into the action more; it is a kind of minor character.

5. Careful motivation of exits and entrances.

6. Extensive and effective use of dramatic irony.

7. Use of prophecies which foreshadow the action and prepare the audience for the dramatic irony.

8. Frequent use of a joyful lyric prior to catastrophe.

9. Use of contrast for character revelation.

10. Situations which force characters to extreme limits.

11. Serious, even severe tone. The spirit of the plays is heroic, Homeric.

Themes And Attitudes

1. Orthodox views of conventional religion. Accepts the infallibility of the Delphic Oracle, for example.

2. Plots are illustrations of great moral principles: supremacy and inscrutability of the gods; faith in a moral order in the universe; suffering as an inherent part of man's condition.

3. Belief in the potential dignity of man.

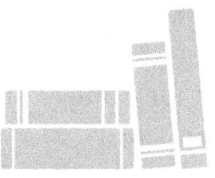

AJAX

BACKGROUND

It is not known when *Ajax* was presented, what other plays were presented with it, or what prize it won. Most scholars believe it to be the earliest surviving play by Sophocles.

Ajax, son of Telamon, is regarded in the *Iliad* as the second most powerful warrior after Achilles. In Homer's other **epic**, the *Odyssey*, Ajax is seen in Hades by Odysseus, but he impressively refuses to speak. The events of *Ajax* occur after the events recorded in the *Iliad* and before those in the *Odyssey*.

When Patroclus fought his last battle in the Trojan War, he was wearing Achilles' armor, which was taken by Hector. Achilles' mother, Thetis (a sea-goddess), had Hephaestus (god of fire, artificer of the gods), make Achilles new armor, which became famous for its superb craftsmanship and pictorial decorations. After Achilles was killed, a contest was held to decide who should inherit this splendid armor. The chief contenders were Ajax and Odysseus. When the Greek leaders awarded the armor to Odysseus, Ajax believed his honor impugned and set out to kill Agamemnon and Menelaus, whom he held responsible. The goddess Athena, long impatient with the pride of Ajax, sent him mad, and he slaughtered the army's cattle and sheep and carried some back to his tent, under the illusion they were the Greek leaders he hated. Sophocles' *Ajax* opens the morning after his attack on the flocks.

CHARACTERS

Athena, daughter of Zeus, patron goddess of Athens; on Greek side in Trojan War; causes Ajax's madness.

Odysseus, one of Greek leaders in the Trojan War; usually characterized as wily and scheming; in *Ajax* a figure of wisdom and prudence.

Ajax, leader of forces from Salamis on Greek side in Trojan War; angry because Achilles' arms were awarded to Odysseus; seeks revenge upon Greek leaders but is frustrated when Athena causes him to slaughter cattle and sheep under the illusion they are the Greek leaders.

Tecmessa, captive woman who is concubine of Ajax.

Teucer, half-brother of Ajax; defies Greek leaders over issue of burying Ajax's body.

Menelaus and Agamemnon, the Atridae, sons of Atreus. Agamemnon was the chief leader of the Greek forces. The war was fought because Menelaus' wife, Helen, had run off with the Trojan prince, Paris.

Chorus, men of Salamis; followers of Ajax.

Messenger.

THE PLAYS OF SOPHOCLES

Mute Characters: Eurysaces, son of Ajax and Tecmessa.

Tecmessa (mute after bringing Eurysaces to his father's body.)

Attendants, Heralds, etc.

SUMMARY

Setting: The Greek encampment near Troy; in front of Ajax's tent. Odysseus stands in front of the tent. The goddess Athena appears from above.

Prologue: Athena asks Odysseus why he is scrutinizing the ground in front of Ajax's tent; perhaps she can enlighten him. Ajax, she says, has just gone inside, his face and hands streaming with blood. Odysseus tells her that the cattle and sheep of the army have been killed during the night and that Ajax was seen in the fields with a bloody sword. Athena explains what had happened: Ajax, believing the award of Achilles' armor to Odysseus to be unjust, sought revenge by killing the Greek leaders. Just outside the tents of Menelaus and Agamemnon, she sent madness upon him, and he attacked the animals instead. Those animals which remained alive, he drove to his tent, and is now inside torturing them. Athena summons Ajax so Odysseus can see his madness and tell the other Greeks. When Odysseus asks her not to call him out, she accuses him of cowardice. He denies being afraid of any sane man, and consents to be a witness only because a goddess asks it.

Ajax comes out of his tent, carrying a blood-stained scourge; he exultantly praises Athena for helping him kill the enemies who kept Achilles' armor from him. He believes Odysseus to be in his tent, and plans to torture him before killing him. Although Athena requests Ajax to be merciful, he refuses and withdraws into the tent.

Comment

The appearance of the mad Ajax exemplifies Sophocles' preference for dramatization rather than narration. In Euripides' *Heracles*, the madness of Heracles is not shown on stage but is narrated in a "messenger-speech."

Athena tells Odysseus that the sight of Ajax's madness should prove the power of the gods, for what man was once more prudent or valiant than Ajax? Odysseus, even though Ajax is his enemy, pities Ajax's hard fate. Odysseus thinks of himself too-being merely mortal, a comparable fate could come to him. Athena tells him Ajax's madness is a warning: never speak proudly before the gods, and never swell with vanity if wealth or strength brings triumph over enemies, for all fortune, good or bad, can be reversed in a single day. The gods love the wise, not the willful.

Comment

Athena has stated one **theme** of the play: hubris is a sin and brings destruction from the gods. (Hubris is the sin of excessive daring, of exceeding the proper limits of man; of aspiring to be like the gods, of being proud.) To avoid hubris is to be wise. In this play the character contrast between Ajax and Odysseus represents the moral contrast between the willful man-guilty of hubris - and the wise man. From a slightly different point of view, the character of Ajax presents a psychological study of wounded honor and its consequences.

Traditionally, the character of Odysseus was that of the wily, clever, scheming man; he is sometimes admirable, sometimes not. Sophocles acknowledges the traditional characterization in the second line of the play when Athena addresses Odysseus and calls him a man who always schemes to gain an advantage over his foes. By the end of the prologue, a highly dignified Odysseus emerges; he is respectful and obedient of Athena, he is afraid of strength when it is directed by an irrational mind, and he pities the hard fate of the man who wants to kill him.

Parodos: The Chorus of men from Salamis, followers of Ajax, enter. They have heard Odysseus' story of Ajax's slaughter and do not believe it. They want Ajax to come out of his tent and deny the talk. Being lowly men, they say they cannot do it themselves - the lowly need the mighty as much as the mighty need the lowly. Even if what Odysseus says is true, surely some god drove him to it; the real Ajax would never go so far in folly.

First **Episode**: Tecmessa, a captive and the concubine of Ajax, enters to lament with the Chorus Ajax's madness. She confirms the truth of what they heard; the proof may be seen inside the tent. The Chorus want to flee in their ships, but Tecmessa tells them that Ajax has recovered. She had been in the tent when he returned from the slaughter, and she saw him torturing and reviling the animals as if they had been men. When his reason began to return, Ajax saw the carnage around him and sank moaning to the ground. He threatened to kill Tecmessa unless she told him what had happened, but she knew little. Now he is sitting among the slain animals, moaning to himself, and refusing food and drink.

Comment

Tecmessa and the Chorus are little characterized and have little significance in the plot, but both are adroitly conceived within the limits of their functions. As followers of Ajax, the Chorus is well motivated for either lamentation, joy, or moral comment. Tecmessa, who loves Ajax, and who has a stake in his fortunes, is more effective than the usual "messenger" for reporting off-stage action.

From within the tent comes the voice of Ajax, calling for Teucer - his half-brother, away on an expedition - and his son, Eurysaces. The leader of the Chorus suggests that the tent be opened; perhaps the sight of his followers will clear his mind. When Tecmessa opens the text, Ajax is revealed, sitting among the slain animals.

Comment

This scene was probably staged with the use of the eccyclema, a movable platform rolled out before the audience. It was used to depict interior scenes in tableau form.

Ajax wants his followers to kill him, saying only death can save his honor now. He will be laughed at for attacking animals. His rage mounts as he thinks that Agamemnon, Menelaus, and, in particular, Odysseus, have escaped his wrath. He knows Athena caused his madness and realizes he is hated by the gods, as well as by his allies, the Greeks, and their enemies, the Trojans. His primary concern is with his honor, and he contemplates various courses of action: if he deserts the Greeks and goes home, he will be despised by his father; if he assaults Troy alone and dies in some glorious exploit, his enemies will be happy. There is, he feels, no alternative to death; if a proud man cannot live nobly, he must die nobly.

Comment

Ajax has clearly learned nothing from his experience; his great pride, which had led him to dispute the award of Achilles' armor, is still unshaken and no element of humility appears. Before assessing Ajax's character and evaluating his words in this scene, two principles of Greek popular morality must be remembered; first, that it was intolerable to be laughed at, and second, that doing harm to one's enemies was as natural as doing good to one's friends. On the other hand, while conventional morality might tremble at the thought of hubris, heroic action almost requires it. Nor is it necessarily contradictory for a writer to admire action which he does not recommend for everyone. Also, when discussing the moral viewpoints in Greek tragedy, it must always be remembered that the plays are not sermons.

Tecmessa pleads that he not talk of dying; he must consider what would happen to her and their son. He does not reply to what she says, but asks that their son be brought in. Holding the boy, Ajax hopes that he'll be happier than his father. Teucer is to be responsible for him, and he is to be given Ajax's shield -the other arms to be interred with Ajax's body. He gives the child to Tecmessa and tells her to go. She has become frightened by his talk and begs, in the name of the gods, that he not forsake them.

He replies that he no longer owes the gods any duty, orders the tent closed upon him, and dismisses Tecmessa.

Comment

This scene is unusual in its use of a child for emotional effect, a device frequently found in Euripides.

First Stasimon: The men of the Chorus lament the long time they have been away from Salamis; now Ajax's madness will bring them more unhappiness. His mother and father will suffer bitterly when they hear of what has happened. Anyone in Ajax's plight would be better off hidden in Hades.

Second **Episode**: Ajax comes out of his tent carrying a sword. He says his misfortunes began when he traded his belt for the sword of Hector he is carrying. His mood appears to be completely changed, and he speaks like a humbled man, vowing to obey the gods and the leaders of the army. He says that hatred for enemies should be limited because they may someday become friends; service for friends should be qualified too because they may become foes. Reassuring Tecmessa that all will be well, he sends her inside the tent and departs.

Second Stasimon: The Chorus sing a joyful song celebrating Ajax's new frame of mind, his piety, and his humility.

Comment

Ajax's speech of repentance and humility-possibly the finest speech in the play-is in fact his farewell to Tecmessa and his army. To be left alone, to avoid being forcibly restrained from suicide, he does not tell them his real purpose. His new piety towards the gods and submission to his leaders are at least an intellectual acknowledgment of the course of wisdom. His earlier decision that only death can preserve his honor is unchanged; his next speech reveals that his hatred of the Atridae ("sons of Atreus," Agamemnon and Menelaus) is also unchanged, but his submission to the gods is apparently sincere. The scene can also be read as a device to deceive the audience, intensifying the dramatic effect of Ajax's suicide.

Having the Chorus misinformed or having them misunderstand the true situation and sing a song of joy just before some catastrophic action is a characteristic Sophoclean dramatic device. The happiness of the Chorus is seen by the audience as dramatic **irony**; it also sharpens the emotional intensity of the following scene by contrast.

Third **Episode**: A messenger enters looking for Ajax. He says Teucer returned from his expedition and was nearly killed by the army for Ajax's mad slaughter of the animals. The leaders finally stopped the violence and save him. Calchas, the seer, then told Teucer that if Ajax left his tent the day after slaughtering the animals, he would never again be seen alive. Calchas also told what proud acts of Ajax had brought down Athena's anger on him: when Ajax left home his father had told him to fight well and always to invoke the help of the gods. Ajax had replied that anyone could win with the gods' help; he would triumph without it. Later, on the battlefield Athena had ordered Ajax to attack the Trojans; he told her to help the other Greeks - no Trojans would get by him. The leader of the Chorus calls Tecmessa out of Ajax's tent to hear the messenger's news. She immediately sends the Chorus out to search for Ajax and to summon Teucer. She takes the child, planning to join the search for as long as her strength holds out.

Comment

An unusual feature of this tragedy is the dismissal of the Chorus from the stage, very well motivated by having Tecmessa send them to search for Ajax. Other technical innovations follow: the scene changes and Ajax commits suicide on stage. Customarily, violent actions are performed off-stage, then revealed by the eccyclema (see General Introduction) or reported by a messenger or other witness.

The scene is now understood to represent a desolate place near the shore (probably by using a different part of the stage). Ajax, alone, has planted his sword in the ground, point up. He prays to Zeus that Teucer may find his body and give him a proper burial, that he die suddenly, and that the Greeks be destroyed. Saying farewell to the sunlight, he falls on his sword.

Second Parodos: Part of the Chorus comes in looking for Ajax and meets with the rest of the Chorus; they sing of their grief at having searched so long and unsuccessfully ("strophe," see comment below). A cry is heard from another part of the stage: Tecmessa has found Ajax's body. To prevent anyone's seeing the body before Teucer arrives to prepare it properly for burial, she covers it. The Chorus sing of the fate of Ajax, which began to work itself out when Odysseus was awarded the arms of Achilles ("antistrophe").

Comment

The construction of the play is unusual at this point because there is a second parodos, or entry of the Chorus. The two parts of the choral song (strophe, antistrophe) are separated by the lines of Tecmessa and the leader of the Chorus. The result is dialogue with interlarded lyrics (epirrhematic construction). Because it is customary to call a choral song a "stasimon" - which separates episodes-only when the song is complete, the lines of Tecmessa are included in the "second parodos."

Fourth **Episode**: The Chorus and Tecmessa lament the death of Ajax. She fears that she will suffer at the hands of the Atridae. They and Odysseus will now laugh at Ajax, but will learn what kind of man they lost when they need him in battle. Teucer enters, and when he learns of Ajax's death, sends Tecmessa to get Eurysaces, lest harm come to him. Uncovering the body, Teucer laments the death of Ajax, wondering how he can now go home to their father, Telamon. Will not Telamon accuse the slave's child, Teucer, of conniving at Ajax's death to inherit the kingdom?

Menelaus enters and immediately forbids the burial of Ajax's body.

Comment

This play (like many of Euripides) falls into two parts. The first part was concerned with the consequences of Ajax's madness. The second part deals with the treatment to be accorded his corpse.

Teucer demands a reason, and Menelaus says that Ajax, had he not been stopped by a god, would have killed many of the Greeks who had welcomed him as a friend. Ajax must serve as an example to those who would act against their leaders; the whole of society would collapse without awe and reverence. Teucer denies that Ajax owed obedience, for he had come to help voluntarily; Menelaus is master only of the Spartans. The leader of the Chorus, who had told Menelaus not to lay down wise precepts and then offer outrage to the dead, now warns Teucer that his harsh words, however just, will cause trouble. Teucer, however, remains adamant; he even goes so far as to accuse Menelaus of intriguing against Ajax when the judges awarded Achilles' armor to Odysseus. Menelaus repeats his order that the body not be buried and, disdaining further argument, departs. Tecmessa and Eurysaces enter; Teucer ceremoniously has the boy kneel by his father like a suppliant while he goes out to dig the grave.

Comment

Tecmessa, although before the audience again, does not speak again. Her role is now played by a "mute actor." The speaking actor who performed her role earlier has changed costumes and appears, probably, as Menelaus. The role of Eurysaces, of course, has been taken by a mute actor throughout the play.

Third Stasimon: The Chorus lament their long years of exile from home; they curse the man who first taught the use of arms in war. War brings man neither joy nor love.

Exodos: Teucer returns, having heard that Agamemnon is on his way. Agamemnon enters and indignantly demands to know why a slave's son like Teucer thinks he can defy the Greek leaders. He tells Teucer to get a free man to speak for him; his barbarian tongue is incomprehensible. Teucer accuses Agamemnon of ingratitude for not remembering Ajax's heroic triumphs in the Greek battles against the Trojans. After pointing out that Agamemnon's birth is no better than his own, Teucer says he'll bury Ajax or die in the attempt.

Odysseus enters and, to the astonishment of Agamemnon, takes Teucer's side. He says that not only was Ajax the most valiant of the Greeks who came to Troy (excepting Achilles), but that it is a wrong against heaven to dishonor the dead, even though one hates them. Odysseus adds that he himself will also die one day, and in a sense serves himself in serving Ajax. Agamemnon goes out, after granting permission, but says that Odysseus will have full responsibility for the funeral. Odysseus plans to assist in the ceremonies, but Teucer feels it would not have pleased Ajax and Odysseus graciously leaves. Teucer sends the men of the Chorus out to make funeral preparations; the remainder help him carry out the body.

Comment

Although this play appears to fall into two parts with the death of Ajax, its formal and thematic unity become evident after the exodos. Odysseus, who has been absent from the stage since the prologue, returns, giving the exodos a formal balance with the opening of the play. His arguments show that the Atridae, if they forbid the burial of Ajax's body, are offending the gods as grievously as Ajax had. Like Ajax, the Atridae follow the course of wisdom with reluctance; their characters, like his, remain narrow, suspicious, and vindictive. Odysseus' philosophical wisdom appears to be the outgrowth of his large-mindedness, which enables him to pity Ajax in the prologue, and to show no rancor when Teucer excludes him from the funeral services.

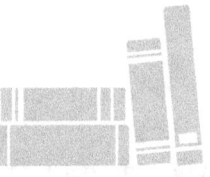

ANTIGONE

BACKGROUND

What other plays were presented with *Antigone* and what prizes it won are unknown. The story of Antigone's attempt to bury her brother's body in defiance of Creon's orders is not recorded in extant **epic** or lyric material. The earliest known account is in Aeschylus' *Seven Against Thebes*. Other incidents in Sophocles' *Antigone* almost certainly his own innovations are the use of Ismene for character contrast to Antigone, the introduction of Teiresias to foretell the consequences of Creon's decision, and the presence of Haemon, who usually dies before Oedipus in the **epic** version (as reported by an ancient commentator on Euripides' *Phoenissae*). This play has always been considered one of Sophocles' best. An ancient story recounts that Sophocles was elected a general in the Samian War (c. 440 B.C.) because of the current admiration for *Antigone*. Two other extant plays of Sophocles deal with events from the Theban cycle of legends: *Oedipus the King* and *Oedipus at Colonus*.

After Oedipus, king of Thebes, exiled himself, his two sons, Eteocles and Polyneices, became Thebes' rulers. They agreed to reign in alternate years, but after the first year Eteocles refused to surrender the throne. Polyneices joined forces raised by

Adrastus, king of Argos, and attacked Thebes. In a duel during the battle the two brothers, Polyneices and Eteocles, killed each other. Creon, their uncle, assumed the throne and ordered that Eteocles be given a hero's honors at his funeral, but that the body of Polyneices, who sinned in attacking his native city, be exposed in the fields. (For further information about the progenitors of Eteocles and Polyneices, see *Oedipus the King* and *Oedipus at Colonus*.)

CHARACTERS

Antigone, daughter of Oedipus; she is determined to give the body of Polyneices a proper burial.

Ismene, sister of Antigone; she believes she can only submit to the law of Creon and refuses to help Antigone.

Creon, king of Thebes, orders that Polyneices' body not be buried.

Eurydice, wife of Creon, commits suicide after her son's suicide.

Haemon, son of Creon and Eurydice; betrothed to Antigone; commits suicide after Antigone does.

Teiresias, blind prophet who foretells consequences of Creon's decision to kill Antigone.

Guard, one of a group sent to prevent the burial of Polyneices' body.

Chorus, Theban elders.

Messenger.

SUMMARY

Setting: In front of the royal palace in Thebes.

Prologue: Antigone has brought her sister, Ismene, outside of the palace to tell her privately the news that Creon has forbidden the burial of their brother Polyneices. Creon gave an honorable burial to their other brother, Eteocles, and Antigone believes the same rites due to Polyneices. She asks Ismene to help bury him, although the punishment for disobeying Creon is death. The prospect of such a fate for herself reminds Ismene of the many misfortunes in her family: of her father Oedipus, who blinded himself; of her mother, Jocasta, who hanged herself; and of her two brothers, who killed one another in a duel just the day before. She tells Antigone they must remember they are women - who should not struggle against men - and that they are ruled by someone stronger - who must be obeyed because of his strength. Antigone argues that by not burying Polyneices they would be dishonoring the gods; and since they will be longer with the dead than the living, they owe the dead more allegiance.

Comment

The necessity for the dead to receive a proper burial is a frequent issue in Greek tragedy (e.g., Sophocles' *Ajax* and Euripides' *Suppliants*). According to Greek religious beliefs, a soul could not immediately enter into its place in the underworld without proper burial. To deny such burial was considered sacrilege. However, under Greek law, certain criminals, such as temple robbers, were denied burial; in some tragedies (e.g., Sophocles' *Electra*) implicit approval is given to denying burial. Such exceptions, however, would serve to reflect shame on Polyneices if he received no burial.

Ismene, with faint hope Antigone will not be discovered, advises her to keep her plan secret; Ismene herself promises to keep it secret. Antigone scornfully tells her to reveal it, and she'll be hated less by Creon. Ismene is hurt, but says she cannot do the impossible - and that no matter what Antigone does or says, she will always love her. They go back inside the palace.

Comment

One of Sophocles' innovations in the story is making Ismene's character a foil to Antigone's. As soon as Ismene hears of Creon's order, she says she can do nothing. She denies that doing nothing dishonors the gods, for she is not a free agent. The status of women was low in Greece, and especially so in Athens, Sophocles' city, and Ismene's sense of the traditional unimportance of women is strong. She has, in short, a "feminine" personality and chooses to stay within the limits that implies.

Antigone, of course, is not acting solely from dedication to an abstract principle. She feels that the edict has been directed toward the two sisters personally: she speaks of the law that "Creon hath set forth for thee and me, - yes, for me" (Jebb translation). Antigone's instinct is to regard the burial as a largely personal matter, as if soldiers were no longer the property of the state when they die, but reverted to their families - to the mourning women. Of course, the matter does not long remain a private one because of Creon's edict. Undoubtedly helping to reinforce Antigone's sense of personal affront is the fact that her brother, father, and grandfather were the previous kings of Thebes. Herself a princess, and the town victorious, how could she expect such vindictiveness from her own uncle, Creon?

Parodos: The Chorus of Theban elders enter to sing happily of the previous day's victory. They have not heard of Creon's edict, and praise Zeus, who enabled the Thebans to triumph over the proud Argive invaders. Only the thought of the two brothers killing one another mars their happiness. They recommend that the temples be visited, that singing and dancing fill the night, and that Bacchus, the god of wine, be their leader.

Comment

Sophocles frequently uses his Chorus to provide an ironic contrast with the mood of the action.

First **Episode**: Creon comes out of the palace and tells the Chorus he summoned them because of their well-known loyalty to the ruling house of Thebes. He announces his decree that Eteocles be given a state funeral and Polyneices' body be left a corpse for birds and dogs to eat. A guard has been stationed over the body to enforce the decree. To indicate the general principles he will follow as their king, he says that a ruler must listen to the best counsels and implement them by action, and that no friend of the ruler should take precedence over his obligations to the state. He requests of the elders that they not side with anyone who breaks his decree forbidding Polyneices' burial. They reply that they are not in love with dying; Creon says that bribery has often ruined men. A Guard-frightened at having to deliver bad news, protesting that he was not guilty and asking "immunity" in advance-says that someone has sprinkled dirt on Polyneices' body and performed other rites over it. There was no evidence of how the person reached the body, nor was there any evidence that animals had come near it. The leader of the Chorus suggests it may have been the gods' doing, but Creon dismisses this out of hand, saying the gods never honor the wicked. Creon believes the guards were bribed. He tells the Guard who brought the news that if the person who violated his edict not be found, the Guard will be tortured and killed. It is sad, the Guard says, when those who judge, judge erroneously. Creon returns to the palace and the Guard goes out.

Comment

Creon's general principle of kingship, that a ruler must serve the state first, is irreproachable. His understanding of that duty in the present case is that the body of a man who attacks his native city must be dishonored. Antigone understands her duty to be the burial of her brother's body, and she invokes the authority of religion. It would, however, be an over-simplification to reduce the **theme** of the play to a conflict between state and religion. For one reason, Creon believes his act to be pious. Perhaps the **theme** is best stated as the conflict between society and tyranny. A tragedy, of course, is not only a moral argument. Interest in the people of the tragedy engages the audience more powerfully than argument alone.

Although the title of the play tells us that the **protagonist** is Antigone, some critics have argued that the **protagonist** is Creon. Certainly he is more complicated and is shown with more sympathy than if he were intended to be seen only a villainous tyrant. Already, in the first **episode**, the audience sees him committed to a course of action which may be impious - the Chorus suggest that the dust on Polyneices' body and the fact that the animals have not touched it are the work of the gods - and the audience sympathetically feels fear for him. His readiness to suspect everyone of bribery, and the Guard's accusation that he is an unjust judge, lose sympathy for him. Such complication of character also serves to maintain suspense because Creon's decisions cannot be anticipated.

First Stasimon: The Chorus sing of the wonder of man, who triumphs over the sea, the land, the animals, and the weather- only Death has not been defeated. Man has created cities, which will survive if man avoids sin. May a sinner never come to Thebes!

Comment

The Chorus' statement is abstract, almost theoretical. It makes no specific application to Creon and gives the effect of withholding judgment.

Second **Episode**: The Guard returns, bringing in Antigone. To the astonishment of the Chorus and of Creon, who comes hurriedly from the palace, he reports having caught her in the act of covering the corpse from which they had just swept the dust of the earlier attempt. He says that a whirlwind of dust had momentarily blinded the guards, but when it passed they say Antigone, who cried aloud when she saw the uncovered body. Then she poured a drink offering and scattered dust on the body. The Guard anxiously requests that he now be freed of the earlier charge of bribery and disobedience; Creon frees him and he leaves.

> Comment

Here and in the earlier **episode**, the Guard is shown as a garrulous coward, preoccupied with his own safety. He is one of the rare comic characters represented in Greek tragedy. (Cf. the Nurse in Euripides' Medea, and the Phrygian Eunuch in his Orestes.)

Antigone proudly admits that she is guilty of disobeying Creon's decree; she obeyed a higher law than any he could pass and is prepared to die. The leader of the Chorus says she is like her father: passionate and unwilling to bend before circumstance. Creon says her insolence knows no bounds, for she not only broke the law but now brags of it. That she is his niece will not stay the punishment; in fact, he holds Ismene equally guilty and orders that she be brought out. Antigone maintains that the Chorus of elders would be on her side if they weren't afraid of Creon's royal power. She brushes aside Creon's argument that she is giving Polyneices, who attacked his own city, equal honors with the brother who defended it.

When Ismene is brought out and Creon accuses her, she accepts the guilt. Antigone will not allow this, saying Ismene is sympathetic only in words. Although Ismene says her life will be nothing without her, Antigone continues to spurn her. Ismene then asks Creon whether he will kill his own son's betrothed, and he replies that his son shall have no evil wife. Creon then orders Antigone and Ismene taken inside and closely watched.

> Comment

This is the first time Creon's son, Haemon, has been referred to in the play, and is an example of Sophocles' adroit use of surprise-in the traditional legend, Haemon was killed by the Sphinx before Oedipus arrived in Thebes.

Second Stasimon: The Chorus sing of the woes of the Labdacidae (descendants of Labdacus: Laius, Oedipus, and Oedipus' children). Once a house has been cursed by heaven, the curse continues to bring evil, generation after generation. Now the last flower of that house is to be destroyed. The power of Zeus is without limit; he lives forever. Man hopes for much, but he is blind. The old saying is true that Fate brings misfortune under the disguise of happiness - then woe descends.

Third **Episode**: Haemon enters and Creon asks him whether he is angry with his father for the sentence passed on Antigone. The son politely replies that he will follow his father's guidance in all matter. Creon is delighted to find Haemon an ideal son. How could he expect the city to obey him if his own family won't? Antigone is a law-breaker and must be punished. Only obedience will preserve cities; laws, whether just or unjust, must be obeyed. The worst disobedience of all is that of a woman; Creon says that if he must fall, let it not be to a woman.

Haemon replies that he has neither the desire nor the skill to deny what his father has said; yet his job is to observe the citizens, listening to what they would say to the king's face, and he wants to offer a useful thought. The citizens say Antigone should be rewarded rather than punished for the piety she has shown. Since a son only wants his father to prosper, Haemon suggests that Creon learn to bend with the wind when necessary. Creon is indignant that a younger man should presume to teach him how to act, that Thebes' citizens should tell him how to rule, and that his son is giving in to a woman. Haemon ambiguously says that if Antigone dies, she will not die alone, and Creon understands it as a threat that Haemon will murder him. He becomes so angry he orders Antigone brought out and killed before Haemon's eyes. Haemon, telling him to rave on, leaves. When Creon tells the Chorus that no one can save the two girls, the leader asks whether he really intends to kill both, and Creon excepts Ismene. Antigone, however, he will have locked in a cave in the wilderness with enough food to absolve the state of her death, according to the custom. Perhaps the gods of Hades whom she loves so much will save her, Creon says.

Comment

Haemon's patience and his deference to his father are the very model of "sweet reasonableness." He puts forth no personal argument, based on his love for Antigone, at all. His concern is entirely for his father and the safety of the state - the very premises Creon himself has based his arguments on.

The modern reader would expect a scene between Antigone and her betrothed to follow, but the Greeks never represented such scenes of tender emotion.

Third Stasimon: The Chorus say that love, the goddess Aphrodite, has triumphed, warping Haemon's mind and causing strife between father and son. When Antigone appears, however, they say they cannot stay within the bounds of loyalty, and break into tears.

Comment

The Chorus maintains a certain kind of dramatic tension by refusing to take an unqualified position on either side. In the third episode, for instance, they felt there was wisdom in the speeches of both Creon and Haemon. They are most consistently distressed by open quarrels, imminent danger, or personal suffering. They are also men, of course, which may limit their sympathy for Antigone.

Fourth **Episode**: Antigone, guarded, comes on stage; her defiant mood has completely changed. She realizes that she is soon to die and laments that she will never be married. She asks the Chorus to bear witness to the unjust law which has caused her death. The Chorus try to console her by saying she has dared much and will die gloriously; her punishment, they say, is actually attributable to her father's sin. (In a passage omitted by some editors as spurious, Antigone says she would not have defied the law for a husband or child, for they could be replaced; but since her mother and father are dead, no brother can ever replace Polyneices. Those critics who consider the lines genuine argue that Antigone is using every possible rationalization in an intensely emotional situation, and that in actuality she probably would make the same sacrifice for a husband or child.) Creon comes from the palace and orders the guards to hurry her away; lamentations never help the doomed, he says.

Comment

Antigone, who earlier in the play seems somewhat cold and fanatical, here displays her humanity and her capacity to suffer. The Greeks represented Hades as an unpleasant place at best; Antigone is not a martyr in the Christian sense.

Fourth Stasimon: The Chorus refer to others who suffered cruel misfortunes: the son of Dryas, the sons of Phineus, and Danae.

Fifth **Episode**: The blind prophet Teiresias, led by a boy, enters. He has come to warn Creon that the unburied body of Polyneices has offended the gods - the sacrifices are not being accepted and the birds of augury scream and fight with rage. Creon accuses him of having accepted bribes to recommend burying Polyneices. Teiresias continues, telling Creon it will not be long before a child of his dies because Creon is keeping from Hades one who belongs there (Polyneices), and is sending to Hades one who belongs in the sunlight (Antigone). Refusing to stay for a reply, Teiresias tells Creon to vent his anger on younger men. After the boy has led Teiresias out, the leader of the Chorus tells Creon that the old prophet has never been wrong. Creon becomes frightened and decides, reluctantly, to take the advice of the Chorus, which is to bury Polyneices and free Antigone. Telling his servants to bring axes, he leads them to the cave holding Antigone.

Comment

At this point the play could turn toward the happy ending of a Euripidean melodrama. Creon becomes pathetic when his humanity is touched by the possibility of his son's death.

Fifth Stasimon: The Chorus sing a hymn of praise to Bacchus and joyfully ask him to come to the aid of the city.

Comment

A joyful choral song just before a **catastrophe** is a characteristic Sophoclean device, used also in *Ajax*, *Oedipus the King*, and *Trachiniae*.

Exodos: A messenger comes in and tells the Chorus that Creon, once blessed for having saved the city of Thebes from attack, by having been its only ruler, and by having princely children, has now lost all. Haemon has committed suicide. Eurydice, Creon's wife, enters, having heard of Haemon's death, and asks the messenger for more information. He says that he had gone with Creon to the body of Polyneices, which, after prayers, was given a proper burial. They then went to the cave where Antigone was imprisoned and were greeted by lamentations from Haemon. Inside they found that Antigone had hanged herself, and Haemon was clinging to her body. When Creon called to him, he cursed his father and drew his sword to kill him, but Creon rushed forward and he missed. Angry with himself, he leaned against his sword, driving it into his side. He died clinging to Antigone's body. Without saying anything Eurydice goes back into the house. The messenger believes she has gone to lament in private, but the Chorus feel her silence to be ominous. The messenger follows her. Creon enters, lamenting the death of his son, admitting it was caused by his own folly. The messenger returns from the house to tell Creon that Eurydice is dead. The doors of the palace are opened and the body of Eurydice is revealed. The messenger says that before she stabbed herself, she cursed Creon for causing the death of both their sons.

Comment

Their other son, Megareus, was one of the seven champions who defended Thebes in Aeschylus' *Seven Against Thebes*. Euripides, in *Phoenissae*, calls him Menoeceus and shows him voluntarily killing himself as the sacrifice the gods demanded for a Theban victory.

Creon acknowledges full responsibility for the deaths of Haemon and Eurydice. He prays to the gods that his own death might come soon to end his suffering.

Comment

In the exodos the suffering of Creon completely overshadows the fate of Antigone, who is hardly mentioned, apart from the description of her death. Throughout the play Creon has been the chief agent; it is he who acts and causes his own suffering, as well as Antigone's. Such arguments support the interpretation that the play is primarily about Creon. On the other hand, it is argued that the suffering of Creon justifies Antigone, reflecting, as it were, a religious illumination of her position. Certainly both Antigone and Creon are honoring the gods in their respective fashions, and whether being wrong makes Creon a tragic figure supplanting Antigone as **protagonist** of the play is debatable.

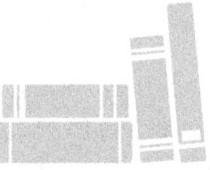

OEDIPUS THE KING

BACKGROUND

There is dispute about the exact date of this play. The dating argument hinges on possible relationships between the plague described in the play and an actual plague in Athens in 430-427 B.C. It is not known what other tragedies were presented in the same contest, but an ancient commentator says that *Oedipus* was awarded second place. If so, the prize was no indication of the play's merits, for Aristotle, in his *Poetics*, praises it very highly, and subsequent generations have taken it as the perfect model of Greek tragedy. Among the more important adaptations of the play are those by Seneca (1st century A.D.), Corneille (1659), Dryden and Lee (1679), Voltaire (1718), and Gide (1931). According to present knowledge, the story of Oedipus and his family was dramatized more than any other legend. At least thirteen Greek dramatist wrote plays on the subject. It is a central part of the Theban cycle of legends, which, as a subject for **epic** poetry, was second in popularity only to the Trojan cycle.

Laius, King of Thebes, was told by a prophet that any child born to him and his wife, Jocasta, would murder him. When a child was born, Laius took him from the nurse's arms, pierced his ankles with a spike, tied them together, and had a servant leave him on Mount Cithaeron to die by exposure. A shepherd from Corinth found him and named him Oedipus, meaning "he of the swollen feet." Taken back to Corinth by the shepherd, Oedipus was raised by King Polybus and his queen, Merope, as their own son. After he had grown up, a drunken man at a banquet said he was not the true son of Polybus. Determined to discover the truth about his parentage, Oedipus consulted the Delphic Oracle. He was sent away from the shrine by the horrified Oracle, who told him he would murder his father and marry his mother. To avoid harming Polybus and his wife in any way, Oedipus decided not to return to Corinth. Arriving at a fork in the road outside of Delphi, he encountered Laius and four attendants, riding in a chariot. A quarrel over the right of way ensued, and Oedipus killed Laius and three of the attendants. Laius had been on his way to Delphi from Thebes to seek help in ridding the city of Sphinx. This monster, with a woman's head, eagle's wings, lion's body, and serpent's tail, had flown to a spot near Thebes and asked every passer-by a riddle: what walks on four feet in the morning, two at noon, and three in the afternoon? Those who could not answer, she ate immediately. Oedipus, on the road from Delphi, when accosted by the Sphinx, answered, "Man, who crawls on all fours in childhood, walks on two feet when grown, and uses a staff when old." The Sphinx, angry and mortified, killed herself. The grateful citizens of Thebes proclaimed him their king, and he married the recently widowed Jocasta, not suspecting she was his natural mother. They had twin sons, Polyneices and Eteocles, and two daughters, Antigone and Ismene. After the children were grown, a plague fell on Thebes, decimating the population. It is at this point that the play begins.

THE MYTH AND RITUAL PATTERN

Myth as a way of ordering human experience was brought to prominence during the late nineteenth and early twentieth centuries by a group known as the Cambridge school of classical anthropologists. From their theories has developed what is now called the "myth method" of literary analysis. The basis of the myth method is the identification of certain pre-eminent types of characters and ritual patterns of experience which compose the action, meaning, and form of the myth. The *Oedipus the King* of Sophocles has become one of the standard examples of this method of analysis. The foundation of the ritual pattern is the concept of universal order which, if disturbed, must be re-established. Often the ritual pattern has to do with seasonal changes and the propitiation of the gods to ensure animal, vegetable, and human fertility or with vegetation rites which have frequently to do with individual growth and development as well as community welfare. This is the basis for the ritual pattern of the Oedipus myth, for it is thought that archaic rituals among primitive peoples gave rise to what we consider classical mythology. Hence, Thebes is beset by a plague which is causing a general cessation of fertility; the gods must be propitiated and universal well-being re-established. The tragedy that follows is an interpretation of the mystery of human destiny. The multitude must have a champion, or hero, so they turn to their king, Oedipus. He fulfills the necessary conditions of the mythical hero, for the circumstances of his birth are unusual and he has achieved triumph and position which enable him to challenge a monumental antagonist-universal disorder. As the oracle provides the clues which the other characters gradually corroborate, it becomes evident that the gods must be propitiated by a sacrifice which is commensurate with the original and subsequent evil doings of mortals. In this case it is Laius' disobedience and Oedipus' subsequent actions. The tragic rhythm lies in the fact that the god-like hero is also to become the scapegoat, or sacrifice for the appeasement of the gods' wrath. (Notice how the Thebans' attitude changes toward Oedipus when his guilt and responsibility are revealed). Thus the Chorus becomes an all-important character in its function as the conscience of the race. However, it is not only Oedipus who suffers, but the Chorus as well, for they have lost their hero. Their suffering along with that of Oedipus accomplishes the necessary purgation of evil and once more universal order is established. The final part of the ritual is the resurrection of the dead hero to a position more exalted than that previously held. In the case of Oedipus it is his forgiveness granted by the gods and the prophecy that wherever Oedipus goes he will be a sacred example and that where he makes his final resting place will also be considered sacred.

A NOTE ON FREUD

To the unwary student, the term "Oedipus complex" as applied to the Freudian theory of psychology is synonymous with, and therefore incorrectly related to, the Oedipus myth in ancient Greek literature. (The Oedipus complex is Freud's name for the purportedly universal hostility all young boys feel for their fathers and the sexual attraction they have for their mothers.) The Oedipus myth dealt with in all its versions certain cardinal problems in human and divine affairs on the basis of what we call "archetypal figures" in literature. The effect of the many literary retellings of the *Oedipus* story has always been primarily the fear and pity aroused in the audience by the representation of actions which are inherently wrong in a moral sense. Freud coined the term "Oedipus complex" on the basis of the power of the original myth. It is known, however, that Freud himself debated as to whether to call the psychological mechanism a "Hamlet" complex or an Oedipus complex. The reason for his choice was that the Oedipus myth provided a basis for more variations on the **theme** than did Hamlet, thus making the Hamlet attitude but one of those variations. Moreover, Hamlet has come to represent indecision, which would have been an irrelevant and misleading **connotation** as far as Freud was concerned.

Confusion arises from overlooking Freud's insistence on the subconscious desire of the boy to model himself after Oedipus. As is plainly the case in Sophocles, Oedipus' misfortune was the result of fate over which he had no control. Freud acknowledged the hand of destiny in the Greek myth and adapted the *Oedipus* narrative because it seemed to him to exemplify what he regarded as true of all men. A careful reading of Freud will further illuminate the many variations of the Oedipus complex which the psychologist worked out and which have virtually nothing to do with the Greek myth in its original form.

CHARACTERS

Oedipus, king of Thebes, who had unknowingly killed his father and married his mother, Jocasta.

Jocasta, queen of Thebes, former wife of King Laius, now wife of Oedipus.

Creon, brother of Jocasta, accused by Oedipus of desiring the throne of Thebes.

Herdsman, formerly in the service of King Laius; sent by Laius to expose Oedipus on the mountain.

Teiresias, blind prophet, foretells what Oedipus will discover.

Priest Of Zeus, spokesman for suppliants in prologue.

Messenger, shepherd from Corinth who rescued Oedipus as a child; announces death of King Polybus.

Second Messenger, reports death of Jocasta.

Chorus, Theban elders.

Mute Perons: group of suppliants; Antigone and Ismene, daughters of Oedipus and Jocasta.

SUMMARY

Setting: In front of the royal palace at Thebes. An altar is covered with branches brought by the suppliants, who stand nearby.

Prologue: Oedipus enters from the central doors of the palace. He has come in person, to inquire the suppliants' reason for appearing before the palace. The Priest of Zeus speaks for them, and he tells Oedipus that, as Oedipus already knows, a plague is devastating the country; the crops, the herds, and the people are dying. They have come to ask his aid, not because they think him a god, but because he appeared to have a god's aid when he rid the city of the Sphinx. Knowing their suffering, Oedipus replies that he has already sent Creon, Jocasta's brother, to consult the Delphic Oracle, and vows to do everything the Oracle requires. The Priest tells Oedipus that he has just been told that Creon is nearby. When Creon enters, Oedipus has him repeat the Oracle's words in front of the crowd of suppliants. Creon says that Apollo, the god for whom the Oracle speaks, has ordered Thebes to drive out, by banishment or bloodshed, the man who killed Laius, for he is now defiling the city. Oedipus immediately asks the circumstances of Laius' death. Creon tells him that Laius had been on his way to Delphi when a band of robbers fell on him and his attendants, killing all but one, who returned and reported what had happened. Oedipus suspects some political intriguers bribed the robbers; otherwise they would not have dared attack the king. Why, he asks was no revenge taken? Creon replies that the city was troubled by the Sphinx at the time, and no one rose to avenge Laius. Oedipus announces that avenging Laius is a worthy and necessary duty; he will do everything in his power to find the slayer, for such a man is a potential danger to the present king, too. He asks the suppliants to rise, and he summons the elders of Thebes to announce to them his intention of trying every possible means of discovering Laius' murderer.

Comment

This prologue contains very little **exposition** of past events. The *Oedipus* story was well known to the audience, and Sophocles takes full advantage of this, not only to make the prologue move rapidly, but for dramatic **irony**. Since the audience knows what has happened to Oedipus in the past-which he will soon discover himself-particularly chilling **irony** attaches to his energetic prosecution of the inquiry and such statements as the one about danger to himself from Laius' murderer.

The character of Oedipus and his success as king of Thebes are established in this opening scene. As John Dryden put it: "Sophocles has taken care to show Oedipus, in his first entrance, a just, a merciful, a successful, a religious prince, and, in short, a father of his country."

Parodos: The Chorus of Theban elders enter. They first express fear of the Oracle, wondering in what way it will affect Thebes. They pray to various gods for release from the plague devastating the land.

First **Episode**: Oedipus assures the Chorus they will find relief from their troubles if they will listen to his words. Having only become a Theban after the crime was committed, he needs their assistance. If the murderer denounces himself, his punishment will only be banishment. Anyone who withholds information will be ostracized from human companionship as the defiler of the city. He utters a curse against the murderer, extending it to include himself should the murderer secretly become an inmate of his house. He adds that even if the Oracle had not plagued the city, it would be his duty, as the inheritor of Laius' throne and wife, to find the murderer. Had Laius had children, there would now be ties between him and Oedipus; because he didn't, Oedipus swears to hunt the murderers as if Laius had been his own father.

Comment

Since Oedipus himself is the murderer, the dramatic **irony** in this scene becomes almost excessive; yet excess is avoided because what he says is consistent with his character as a man and as king, and with what the townspeople expect.

The leader of the Chorus suggests that Teiresias, the prophet, be consulted for information the Oracle did not give: the name of the murderer. Oedipus says that, on a suggestion of Creon,

Teiresias has already been summoned. He is surprised that he has not arrived.

> Comment

As in the prologue (with Creon's arrival) Sophocles uses the awkward device of having a person arrive immediately after someone says the person is late. (In the prologue, of course, this device is used to establish the idea that Oedipus was forehanded by sending to the oracle before others suggested it.)

The information that Creon suggested consulting Teiresias prepares for Oedipus' later accusation of Creon as a political intriguer. In the prologue too, Oedipus suspected political intriguers of preventing the investigation of Laius' murder.

Oedipus welcomes Teiresias as the savior of the state, saying that helping others is the noblest task of man. Teiresias does not respond to Oedipus' praise with any enthusiasm. He sadly says that wisdom is a dreadful thing when it brings no profit to the wise, and he requests leave to return home. He says that since Oedipus did not speak in the past, he, Teiresias, will not speak now. Oedipus takes this refusal as an insult to himself and the state, being convinced that Teiresias knows the truth. His anger mounts, and he accuses Teiresias of planning the death of Laius. Angered himself, Teiresias retorts that Oedipus is the slayer. Because he believes the accusation to be no more than angry retaliation, Oedipus challenges Teiresias to repeat it, which he does, adding that Oedipus is living in shame with his nearest of kin. Oedipus taunts the blind seer with being maimed in ear, in wit, and in eye, and says he can never harm any man. He accuses Creon of instigating Teiresias' words. Although he acts like a friend, Creon is secretly envious of the king's prerogatives and seeks them for himself. Teiresias is a fraud because he could not answer the riddle of the Sphinx; both he and Creon are envious of the stranger who could. Teiresias, in self-defense, reveals the whole of his prophecy, saying the murderer is an alien sojourner who will be found a native Theban; a blind man who now has sight; the murderer of his father; and at once son and husband with his wife, and the brother and father of his children.

Comment

One **theme** of this play is the **irony** of circumstance. In this first scene, for instance, Teiresias' reluctance to speak, in deference to Oedipus' feelings (perhaps following the maxim that prophecy is misery too soon given), ironically leads to Oedipus' anger and the truth-but because spoken in anger, the truth is not believed. Another **irony**, effectively linked to the action of the play, is that of the blind man who sees and the seeing man who is blind-Oedipus, now only metaphorically blind, later literally blinds himself. The first **episode** also shows the other side of Oedipus' character: he is suspicious, perhaps because he is a foreigner, and he is hot-tempered. His temper explains his behavior when insulted on the road to Thebes, showing his character then and now to be consistent. These faults comprise his "tragic flaw" and are assisting causes of his misfortune.

    First Stasimon: The Chorus sing of the murderer, wondering who he can be. His flight, they say, had better be fast, for Apollo is pursuing him, and behind Apollo come the dread Fates. The Chorus wonder how to take the words of Teiresias, and they are filled with foreboding. They know of no enmity between the ruling houses of Corinth and Thebes, and they know of no way to test the words of a seer. They know Oedipus to be a good king and will never believe Teiresias until they see some confirmation of his words.

Comment

This choral ode expresses the ambiguities of the Greek attitude toward seers. One of the greatest technical problems Sophocles faced in his play was avoiding a premature discovery of the truth by Oedipus. In the first **episode**, Sophocles shows Teiresias telling the truth, but in a situation where it was distrusted as angry rhetoric. In this ode the Chorus weigh Oedipus' past reputation for wisdom more heavily than Teiresias reputation as a seer. They acknowledge that one man may be superior to another in his knowledge of secret things, but that there is no sure test of prophecies.

Second **Episode**: Creon has heard of Oedipus' charges against him and comes to deny them. When Oedipus sees him, he is amazed at Creon's boldness in facing the man whose crown he wants to steal. Oedipus says that had Teiresias been telling the truth, he would have told it years before; telling it now only proves that Creon put him up to it. Creon says he has no reason to want the throne-he has all the honor and influence of a kingly position without the danger and unhappiness. It is wrong to make random accusations, Creon says. That he reported the words of the Oracle correctly can be confirmed by going to Delphi. If any evidence of a plot with Teiresias is discovered, Creon promises to condemn himself. Oedipus does not believe him and says he must be executed. In the midst of their quarrel, Jocasta comes from the palace, and pleads with them not to increase the troubles of Thebes. The Chorus ask Oedipus not to kill Creon on the basis of an unproved accusation; they swear they have no ulterior motive for this request, and Oedipus sullenly yields to them.

Comment

Although the Creon here is "historically" the same Creon in *Antigone*, his character is completely different. There he is a tyrant, jealous of his prerogatives, suspicious, and easily angered. Here he is wise, patient, and cheerfully content with a high but not the highest position in the land.

Creon leaves, and the Chorus urge Jocasta to take Oedipus into the house. She, however, wants to know why Oedipus has quarreled with Creon, and he repeats Teiresias' words, adding that Creon must have instigated them. Jocasta, confident that she can give the lie to Teiresias, tells Oedipus the prophecy that Laius was to die by the hand of his own son, which he prevented by exposing his only child on a mountainside to die. Further, Laius was actually killed by robbers where three highways meet. Therefore, she says, the old prophecies were wrong. Jocasta's reassurances fail - the mention of three highways wakens a memory in Oedipus. He asks their exact location, the date of Laius' death, a description of him, and how many men were with him. The answers cause him great distress, and he asks what became of the man traveling with Laius who returned to tell what happened at the crossroads. When the man came back, she says, and found Oedipus reigning instead of Laius, he asked to be sent to the country, to be far from the city. Oedipus orders the man brought to the palace.

Comment

Jocasta's speech is one of several in the play which are motivated by a desire to bring good news, and which in fact bring catastrophic news.

Jocasta asks him why her words have so upset him. He tells the story of his upbringing as the son of Polybus and Merope, and of his consulting the Oracle. He says that at the crossroads she described, he was insulted by a herald, whom he struck. When the chariot passed, the old man riding in it hit him on the head. Enraged by such treatment, Oedipus killed them all. No man, Oedipus says, is more miserable than he, for he has banished himself if the stranger was even a relative of Laius. He has polluted the bed of Laius with the hands that killed him; he will be driven from Thebes to fulfill the old prophecy that he would marry his mother and kill his father - and Oedipus names him - Polybus. Jocasta tells him to rest assured that he is not guilty - there was no reason for Laius' servant to have lied about the group of robbers. And even if he should alter his story a little, Oedipus should not worry about prophecies - the one that Laius would be killed by his own son was certainly wrong.

Comment

This long **episode** actually contains three scenes: (1) the quarrel between Oedipus and Creon; (2) the intervention of Jocasta and the Chorus in Creon's behalf, and the departure of Creon; (3) Jocasta's information about the murder, and the fears of Oedipus. By putting the three scenes in a single **episode**, the complication of the Creon-Oedipus quarrel is kept from becoming an excessively prominent subplot. The choral lyrics also break up the repetition of the iambic lines of dialogue (in the Greek) in the two strophes and antistrophes.

Second Stasimon: The Chorus hope that they themselves may always obey the laws of heaven. Tyranny is caused by insolence, and insolence by too much wealth or too great a triumph: but those who presume too much are finally hurled down by the gods. May an evil doom seize those who perform unholy deeds. No more will they go to shrines, they say, if the old prophecies concerning Laius are not fulfilled. The gods are no longer respected by man.

Comment

The Chorus' first comment refers to Oedipus' tyrannous accusation of Creon without evidence. Their other comments generalize the implications of Jocasta's denial of the truth of oracles. Sophocles, unlike Euripides, never attacks traditional religion; he specifically supports the Delphic Oracle and Apollo, both of whom were especially disliked by Euripides.

Third **Episode**: Jocasta comes out with branches and incense for the altar. She says that she cannot quiet Oedipus, and she prays that Apollo will rid the city of its uncleanness and thus relieve the citizens of their fear.

Comment

This orthodox prayer of Jocasta removes some of the Chorus' earlier stigmatization of her as a skeptic; it also has the fearful **irony** that its answer will bring the unhappiness she is trying to prevent.

A messenger comes in looking for Oedipus. From him Jocasta hears that King Polybus has died and that the people of Corinth want Oedipus to be their king. She joyfully sends a servant for Oedipus, who will now be relieved of his fear of killing his father.

> Comment

Again Sophocles uses the device of having a character mistakenly feel joy just before some catastrophic misfortune occurs. From this same messenger Jocasta learns, by the end of the **episode**, the information which leads her to commit suicide.

When he hears the messenger's news, Oedipus agrees with her that oracles are indeed worthless. Yet, he says, need he not fear his mother's bed? Jocasta replies that man has clear foresight of nothing; he is ruled by ups and down of Fortune; it is best to live without attempting to foresee the future.

> Comment

Jocasta's statement that men should live at random denies the basis of serious Greek thinking, which maintained that the universe was governed by law. Jocasta would hold that the universe was chaotic and irrational-without discoverable order.

Jocasta tells Oedipus not to worry about the prophecy of wedlock with his mother: many men dream of such things and are only happy if they ignore them.

> Comment

This is the only reference in the play to what Sigmund Freud has called the "Oedipus complex." Freud was interested in analyzing the subconscious desire to commit incest with his mother, which is manifestly not the case with Oedipus. (See "A Note on Freud," above.)

Oedipus is not reassured. The messenger asks him for more information about the Oracle, and he hears the old prophecy. He asks Oedipus whether hearing of Polybus' death did not make him happy. Oedipus replies that it did and promises him a reward. The messenger says that was his reason for coming; he hoped to gain preferment when Oedipus became king of Corinth. Oedipus says he will never go near his parents, and the messenger, believing he is bringing more good news, tells Oedipus he was not the child of Polybus and Merope. The messenger, while watching his flocks, found Oedipus on a mountainside, his ankles pinned together, "Found" is not an accurate description, Oedipus learns of further questioning, for he was given the child by another shepherd-one from the house of Laius.

> Comment

Again good news leads to **catastrophe**. The messenger, who was good-hearted enough to have accepted the abandoned child from a stranger years before, who watched him raised as his monarch's child, and who brought him the news that he has inherited a kingdom, humanly anticipates, and speaks of, some great reward when Oedipus ascends the throne of Corinth. When the full meaning of his words is known, his hopes fall with Oedipus'. One aspect of Oedipus' fate is that no man's fate is exclusively his own.

As a result of the messenger's information, Oedipus's interest shifts from the search for Laius' murderer to the search for his own identity. To the audience, of course, the two searches are the same.

The messenger does not know whether or not be shepherd who gave him Oedipus still lives, but the men of the Chorus say he is the same man Oedipus summoned earlier-who had been with Laius at the crossroads. Jocasta begs him to carry the search no further, and Oedipus believes she is afraid he'll discover he was basely born. Her despair at what he will discover is too great for her to argue with him, and she goes inside. Oedipus says he must find out who his parents are, however lowly born he may have been. He has always considered his mother to be the goddess Fortune, who brings good.

Third Stasimon: In a brief and joyful song, the Chorus sing of Mount Cithaeron, the nurse and mother of Oedipus. They speculate playfully about which god and goddess might have been his parents.

Comment

A joyful song, ironical in its effect just before the **catastrophe**, is a favorite device with Sophocles.

Fourth **Episode**: The herdsman comes in and is recognized by the messenger from Corinth as the man who gave him the child Oedipus. The herdsman is extremely reluctant to admit he save the child. After close questioning by Oedipus, he reveals that the child was the son of Laius and Jocasta, and that he, out of pity, gave him to the messenger to be reared as a fosterson. Oedipus, realizing that all the prophecies have been proven true, says he will no longer see the light of day and rushes into the place.

Comment

The herdsman, like the messenger, has in his past been motivated by pity and acted in good faith. Like Oedipus, who also tried to avoid his fate by leaving Corinth, they lacked the completeness of information necessary for avoiding catastrophe.

The herdsman, who would have been reluctant to reveal he saved the child because it was in disobedience of Laius' order, learns immediately on his entrance that the child is Oedipus. He already knows that Oedipus killed Laius because he was the only witness. This explains why he asked to leave the palace and go to the country when he saw that Oedipus was king. His lie, that a band of robbers had attacked Laius, served the double purpose of preventing him from seeming a coward in the eyes of the Thebans, and of indicating to Oedipus that he would not betray him. The herdsman, of course, did not know that Oedipus was ignorant of the fact that Laius was king of Thebes.

Fourth Stasimon: The Chorus say that man's life is a shadow. Happiness is only an appearance which falls away. Oedipus' fate is a warning to call no man blessed, for he won prosperity, freed the city of the Sphinx, released the city from death, and became king of Thebes. Yet whose story is now more grievous; whose fortunes are more reversed? The men of the Chorus wish they had never seen him; he once gave them life but now he brings darkness.

Comment

The Chorus here, while lamenting the particular fate of Oedipus, also generalize it as typifying the condition of all men.

Exodos: A second messenger comes out of the palace with the report that Jocasta has hanged herself. She had rushed into her room, closed the doors, and bewailed her marriage to her own son. When Oedipus rushed in, he called for a sword, then sought his wife. With a shriek he broke down the doors to Jocasta's room and saw her hanging by the neck. When she had been taken down, he ripped from her dress the golden brooches she was wearing. With them, he gouged out his eyes, saying they would no more look on the horrors he has committed, on those they should never have seen. Now Oedipus desires to appear before the people, banish himself from the land, and curse his own house.

The doors of the place open and Oedipus comes out, helped by attendants, bloody stains on his face and beard. With the Chorus, he laments the sins of his life, wishing he had died as a child on Mount Cithaeron. Blinding himself has saved him the shame of having to look at his father and mother in Hades, or his children born in sin. He asks to be led away as quickly as possible.

Oedipus' Punishment: One of the larger issues raised by this play is that of Oedipus' punishment. The exact basis for such a tragic fate has been debated by generations of scholars. Most agree, however, that Oedipus incurs his fate for two indirectly related reasons: (1) because of the Oracle who decreed that Laius should be killed and superseded by a son who would marry his widow and be disgraced; (2) because of Oedipus' own pride and individualism which prevent him from submitting himself to tradition. The Greeks believed that although innocence was an individual matter, guilt was shared and inherited. (Compare the Bible's statement that "the sins of the fathers descend upon the sons for seven generations.") Thus, Oedipus is the inheritor of his father's guilt. For Laius, cursed by Pelops for sinning against his host's son, was forbidden by the Delphic Oracle to beget children lest he be destroyed by them. Laius' failure to deny himself the joys of fatherhood caused the prophecy to come true. Thus, Oedipus as an instrument of his father's punishment is carrying out the Oracle's prophecy and becomes the instrument of his own doom. Consequently, his guilt is inherited and then shared. However, his insolent pride increases the magnitude of his tragedy. A basic Greek concept is also demonstrated here - that even the mightiest can fall. Oedipus' skepticism contributes to his own undoing, as can be seen in his attitude toward Teiresias. Thus, Oedipus inflicts upon himself a punishment which he deems fitting to the crime on all accounts.

It must also be kept in mind that the action of the gods is very important in this play. For what they have ordained they will carry out. It may well be that Oedipus is the instrument of both human and divine justice. The general lesson to be learned is that man must be moderate in his prosperity and never exploit his good fortune for the gods can at will destroy it. This concept is an important part of the Greek notion of the "Golden Mean" - moderation in all things.

Creon's approach is announced by the leader of the Chorus; Oedipus is ashamed to face him, having been so unjust. Creon says he has not come to mock Oedipus, or reprove him for any past error. He tells the attendants to take Oedipus inside rather than expose such a polluted man to the gaze of all. Oedipus asks Creon to cast him out of the land with all possible speed, but Creon intends to learn exactly what the gods want done.

Oedipus asks him to give a proper burial to Jocasta; to keep Oedipus outside Thebes as long as he lives; and to care for his two daughters. His sons, he says, are grown men can care for themselves. Before he leaves, Oedipus asks that Antigone and Ismene be brought out, and Creon says he has already arranged this, knowing how much Oedipus loves them. When they come out, he expresses his hope that they will have a better life than he, but is afraid they will be shunned, and that no man will want to marry them. Reluctantly leaving them, Oedipus is led out. The Chorus sing of Oedipus, once mighty, now the lowest of men: no man, they say, can be counted happy until he has finished all his days.

Comment

The exodos allows time for the full effect of the tragedy to be impressed on the audience. The unhappy future of Oedipus and his daughters is hinted at, but no mention of specific misfortunes is made. The presence of Oedipus' two daughters adds pathos to the scene, and, in his last appearance, reminds us of Oedipus' essential dignity.

TWO MODERN ADAPTATIONS

Because the Greek myths so closely represent human problems, they have served as a standard thematic basis for many plays, poems, and stories from ancient times to the present. Two important modern adaptations are *Oedipe* (Oedipus) by André Gide (1931) and *Mourning Becomes Electra* by Eugene O'Neill (1929-1931). Both plays are essentially modern in attitude, but both have retained the essential thematic conflict of their ancestors. It is interesting to compare the presentations of

Sophocles to those of a contemporary Frenchman or American and to see the ways in which their works both differ and remain similar. We will examine Gide's play here, and consider O'Neill's after discussing Sophocles' *Electra*.

Oedipe: The first aspect of Gide's adaptation of *Oedipus the King* that will probably arrest the student is the personality of Oedipus. As Gide presents him, Oedipus is a modern, highly rational man, one of our contemporaries. Unlike the elevated language with which we are familiar in other translations of the ancient drama, the language used by Oedipus and the other characters is more natural to our ear. Although it is somewhat formal and contains brilliant rhetorical passages, it is not the high poetry of the Greek theater. By means of the modernized prose speeches we are able to discern much more of Oedipus' personality. He is revealed as a man who is skeptical of all supernatural forces, particularly religious ones. Gide's Oedipus prides himself on being his own law on the basis of his unknown parentage; with no tradition to follow, he evolves a tradition of his own with each action he takes. He embodies a guiltless, totally self-responsible attitude which is much like the existentialistic philosophy of Jean-Paul Sartre. However, like the Sophoclean Oedipus, Gide's character is eager to solve the mystery of Laius' death and to alleviate the sufferings of the plague-stricken Thebans. To this end he devotes most of his energies in the play. Yet we are able to detect a much more personal interest in the pursuit of his goal than the more abstract fidelity to justice that is displayed by the Sophoclean character.

Other interesting features of Gide's play include the absence of the herdsman, the introduction of Oedipus' children into much of the action, the large part given to Creon, the skeptical attitude of all the characters toward Teiresias, and the highly rationalistic attitude of all the characters toward the final

catastrophe. The main effect of these changes introduced by Gide is to make the play a conflict of ideas, a more intellectualized drama than that of Sophocles. Getting to know the four children of Oedipus enables us to see the interrelationships of the family and the total effect that Oedipus' individualistic philosophy has had on them. Whereas in the ancient play we often label Oedipus' tragic flaw "hubris," or pride, we see it here in its modern manifestation of individualism versus traditionalism, or as belief in self above all else. In Gide's play Oedipus' **catastrophe** is then the loss of self, which is a highly important concern of modern man.

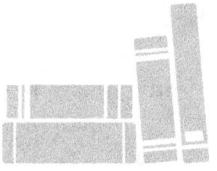

ELECTRA

BACKGROUND

The date of Sophocles' *Electra*, as well as Euripides', is uncertain. A great deal of critical writing has debated which play influenced the other, but no certain sequence has been proved. Sophocles follows the main lines of Aeschylus' *Choephoroe*, with the following changes:

1. The role of Electra is greatly expanded.

2. Orestes' nurse does not appear.

3. Chrysothemis and Pedagogus are added.

4. The scene of recognition and reunion is expanded.

5. The dream of Clytemnestra is different, and differently treated.

6. Agamemnon's grave is not before the audience.

7. Orestes, as a child, has been sent away by Electra.

8. Orestes does not report his own death, and the suspicions of Clytemnestra are not aroused.

9. Clytemnestra, rather than Aegisthus, is slain first.

Aeschylus regards the slaying of Clytemnestra as an evil but necessary act; Euripides condemns it; Sophocles condones it. All are agreed that the slaying of Aegisthus is justified.

When King Agamemnon returned to his home in Argos after the end of the Trojan War, he brought with him as his concubine, Cassandra, a Trojan Princess. The day he returned, Clytemnestra and Aegisthus killed him and Cassandra, *Electra* takes place several years later.

CHARACTERS

Orestes, son of Agamemnon and Clytemnestra, away from home since a child.

Electra, sister of Orestes, who has lived at home, outspoken in her antagonism to Clytemnestra and Aegisthus.

Chrysothemis, sister of Orestes who has behaved so as to please her mother and Aegisthus.

Clytemnestra, wife of Agamemnon; mother of Orestes, Electra, and Chrysothemis.

Aegisthus, lover of Clytemnestra.

Old man, formerly the pedagogus, or tutor, of Orestes.

Chorus, women of Mycenae.

Mute Persons: Pylades, friend of Orestes; handmaiden of Clytemnestra.

SUMMARY

Setting: In front of the palace of Agamemnon in Mycenae, a city of Argolis, in the Peloponnesus.

Prologue: The Tutor addresses Orestes, telling him that he is now at the home of his ancestors, from which his sister Electra had asked the Tutor to take him after his father, Agamemnon, was killed. He has been raised to be the avenger of his father. They must now take counsel and act quickly, for the sun has risen and they might be seen from the house. Orestes thanks the Tutor for his many years of loyalty and tells him what instructions were given by the Oracle of Apollo at Delphi. Orestes, the Oracle said, was to come without the aid of an army and personally take his vengeance. The plan of Orestes is for the Tutor to go into the house, where he will not be recognized because he has grown old and gray. He is to say he is from Phocis, one of Clytemnestra's allies, tell them Orestes was killed in a chariot race, and find out what is happening in the house. Orestes and Pylades will go to the tomb of Agamemnon, as the Oracle ordered, to leave a lock of Orestes' hair and an offering. They will return with an urn they have hidden in the woods, saying it holds Orestes' ashes. Orestes says that reporting his death is not necessarily a bad omen for him; it is a way of entering a new life. He prays briefly for success and is about to go out when moans are heard from the house. Orestes thinks it might be Electra and wants to wait, but the Tutor urges them to follow the commands of Apollo and make their sacrifices immediately.

They have no sooner gone than Electra emerges from the house, clad in ragged clothes. She addresses the sunlight and air, for they have often heard her lamentations for Agamemnon. She vows to pour her curses on Clytemnestra and Aegisthus as long as she lives. She invokes the dread avenging Furies to help her by sending Orestes back.

Comment

In this brief prologue, Sophocles not only outlines the situation and lays the groundwork for the later intrigue, but contrasts the motives and characters of Orestes and Electra. Orestes enters in the name of Justice, hopefully and actively pursuing his aim. Electra's motive is more personal, her tone, lamentation. By adroitly moving Orestes off the stage, Sophocles shows us Electra alone - and isolation has long been her situation. The anticipated joy of their reunion is delayed for the audience.

Parodos: The Chorus of Mycenaean women enter and try to console Electra. She begs them to go away and let her rave as she chooses. They do not deny the justice of her cause, and they are well-meaning. They remind Electra that she is not the only mortal to have suffered. Why can't she bear it as calmly as her sisters, Chrysothemis and Iphianassa?

Comment

According to one of the legends Sophocles followed, Agamemnon and Clytemnestra had four daughters: Iphigenia, who was sacrificed at Aulis before the Trojan War began, Electra, Chrysothemis, and Iphianassa. In other versions, Iphigenia and Iphianassa are variant names for the same person.

Electra, in a lyrical interchange with the Chorus, says that it is wrong to forget a parent's death. The Chorus and Electra both long for the return of Orestes, but Electra is afraid Orestes has forgotten them. He may yearn to be there, as she has heard, but he has never brought himself to act. The Chorus urge that Electra leave her quarrel to Zeus-to remember her foes but forget her excess of wrath. Time can heal, and Orestes will return.

Electra says the best part of her life has already gone; she is without a champion and without children, but serves in the house of her father like a slave. The Chorus say that it was indeed a piteous death Agamemnon suffered while he sat at the welcoming banquet. The lust of Clytemnestra and Aegisthus was the cause.

Comment

This song of lamentation (kommos) between Electra and the Chorus not only expresses lyrically the mood of Electra, but it also introduces Chrysothemis and prepares for the attitude she will take.

First **Episode**: Electra becomes quieter and asks the Chorus to bear with her. How else could they expect a noble woman to behave, having day after day to see the calamities in her father's house, having to live with her father's murderers and be ruled by them? Aegisthus sits on her father's throne, wears his clothes, and lies in her father's bed with her father's wife. Clytemnestra actually celebrates the day she killed Agamemnon by singing, dancing, and making sacrifices. She taunts Electra for thinking no one else ever lost a father, and threatens her for having sent Orestes away.

Comment

In this speech of Electra's, the conditions of her daily life are reported as seen through her eyes, not Sophocles'. Her estimation of Aegisthus as a man who needs the help of women to fight his battles is wide of the mark. She has insight into the effect of her attitude on herself, however, realizing that she must seem difficult to her friends, the Chorus, and that she has chosen to follow, from necessity, "evil ways."

The Chorus ask whether Aegisthus is in the palace now, and Electra says that if he were, she would not have been able to get outside.

Comment

The questions of the leader of the Chorus elicit the information that Aegisthus is out of the way - important for Orestes' plot - and that he is a tyrant who keeps a close watch over his household. Electra, in her long speech just before has maligned him - and underestimated him.

They ask whether Orestes is expected soon; she replies that he is apparently incapable of acting as swiftly as she did when she had him taken away.

Chrysothemis comes out of the palace, richly dressed and carrying offerings. She is surprised to see Electra outside complaining in public again. She herself admits that Electra is right, but believes it best to behave with discretion in troubled times, especially since she is without the power to hurt those she hates.

Electra despises Chrysothemis' attitude and tells her either to help avenge her father, or to forget about him. She has persistently refused to help Electra and even tries to dissuade Iphianassa. What good would it do Electra to stop her laments? For a little food and rich clothes should she give up the pleasure of annoying Clytemnestra and Aegisthus? Chrysothemis has made her choice: she might have been her father's child, but has chosen to be her mother's. The leader of the Chorus urges that the two sisters should each take a little advice from the other.

Chrysothemis replies that she is accustomed to Electra's talk, and wouldn't have mentioned it except that she has heard Aegisthus plans to lock her in the dungeon outside the city, where no one can hear her. Electra replies that she hopes he hurries; then she can get away from the whole family.

Comment

Like the Chorus, Chrysothemis serves as a foil to Electra, by contrast sharpening the outlines of her character. Chrysothemis is in the same position as Electra but is less sympathetic than the Chorus. Her announcement that Aegisthus is about to take action against Electra shows that her denunciations of him have not been without their effect, and that they are not mere self-indulgence. Greater urgency is given to Orestes' return, and the pace of the play's action is accelerated.

Having given her news, Chrysothemis prepares to go on her errand, which Electra learns is to place offerings on Agamemnon's tomb for Clytemnestra. The cause was some dream, Chrysothemis says, and Electra, immediately appreciating the unexpectedness of such a gesture from Clytemnestra, joyfully asks for more information. Chrysothemis says that in the dream Agamemnon appeared, took the scepter now carried by Aegisthus, and planted it by the hearth. A bough grew from it and cast a shadow over the whole land. Chrysothemis says she has heard no more, except that the dream frightened Clytemnestra. Electra tells her not to take Clytemnestra's sacrifice to the tomb, but to take her own and Electra's. The Chorus agree with Electra, and Chrysothemis says she will do what they say, but she begs them not to tell anyone or she will be punished.

Comment

Electra is so intent on revenge that she hails the dream as a good omen before she hears what it is, but curiously attempts no interpretation or comment on it.

First Stasimon: The Chorus say that Justice will come soon to avenge Electra. The dream of Clytemnestra is a reassurance that neither Agamemnon nor the axe which killed him are forgetful of the crime. The Furies will come for revenge; the guilty ones have been driven by their lust to an evil marriage. The Chorus say the land has been accursed ever since Pelops betrayed Myrtilus.

Comment

The reference here is to Orestes' great-grandfather, Pelops, who won a chariot race, a bride, and a kingdom, by having his opponent's charioteer, Myrtilus, damage his opponent's chariot. Pelops had promised, if he won, to give Myrtilus half the kingdom, but treacherously killed him after the race.

Second **Episode**: Clytemnestra comes out of the palace. She says that Electra wouldn't dare be outside repeating her complaints if Aegisthus were there. Clytemnestra denies having insulted Electra; she is merely forced to defend herself from false accusations. Of course she killed Agamemnon, she says, but she was only the instrument of Justice, avenging his sacrifice of Iphigenia at Aulis.

Comment

After the Greeks decided to attack Troy, the Greek forces gathered in their ships at Aulis. Favorable winds, which would enable them to depart, were withheld. The prophet Calchas said that the goddess Artemis was angry with Agamemnon, who was in charge of the expedition, and would not grant the desired winds unless he sacrificed his daughter, Iphigenia, to her.

Clytemnestra argues that Agamemnon had no right to sacrifice her daughter. Wasn't the war being fought to get back Helen, Menelaus' wife? And didn't Menelaus have two children? They should have been sacrificed, unless the gods had some strange desire for Clytemnestra's offspring.

Electra replies that, regardless of the cause, killing her husband was evil. Her real reason, anyway, was lust for

Aegisthus. Further, Electra says, Clytemnestra has the whole story of the sacrifice wrong. What had actually happened was that Agamemnon was once in a grove of trees sacred to Artemis. There he saw a stag, shot it, and later boasted about it. Artemis was angry that one of her sacred creatures was killed, and held up the fleet from going either to Troy or back home in order to force the sacrifice she wanted from Agamemnon. Besides, Electra argues, even if Clytemnestra's version is correct, by what right does she take the law into her own hands? If she intends to establish the principle that blood must be shed for blood, she is the next to be killed. And if Clytemnestra is so jealous to protect her children, why does she now live with Aegisthus, punish Electra, and fail to welcome Orestes home?

Clytemnestra asks the Chorus how she can be expected to care for a daughter who can speak to her mother in such a manner. Electra admits that her behavior is unseemly and that she is, appearances notwithstanding, ashamed of it; but a base mother has taught her base deeds. Her nature, she says, is similar to Clytemnestra's. Clytemnestra requests Electra to be quiet for a minute, for she has come out to make a sacrifice to Apollo.

At the altar, Clytemnestra makes her offering and prays to Apollo. She says that her words are obscure because she is not among friends. Referring to her dream, she asks that it be fulfilled if for her good; if for her harm, let it recoil on her enemies. She prays that Apollo frustrate any attempt to hurl her from the throne and end her happiness.

Comment

The **irony** of Clytemnestra's prayer lies in the fact that she prays to the very god who sent Orestes to kill her. The audience knows that the very opposite of her prayer will be answered only too swiftly.

The Tutor of Orestes enters, posing as a messenger from Phocis. He announces the death of Orestes; Electra wails that she is lost, but Clytemnestra tells her to mind her own business and asks the Tutor for more details.

In a brilliant fabrication, the Tutor tells a story of the Delphinian games. On the first day Orestes won not only the foot race, but every contest held. He was cheered by everyone as the son of the famous Agamemnon. He entered the chariot race too, and started off with the others at the blast from a trumpet. At each end of the course he barely grazed the marking pillars with his axle, so skillfully did he check the inside horse and give rein to the one on the right. On the seventh round one driver's horses ran away, crashing into another chariot, and other chariots piled into the wreck. Only an Athenian and Orestes were left, and Orestes brought his team on a line with the other. First one and then the other was ahead, until Orestes cut a turn too short. The axle of his chariot was broken, and he became tangled in the reins of his frenzied horses. A cry of pity arose from the spectators, and when his horses were finally caught, his body was unrecognizable. The remains were burned on a pyre; his ashes are being brought from Phocis in an urn.

Clytemnestra wonders whether to call this news happy, or bad but profitable. Despite herself, she is unhappy that her son is dead; yet now she is freed from his threats after years of apprehension. Electra laments the loss of her hopes, and invokes heaven; Clytemnestra says heaven has already answered the prayer it wanted to answer. She tells the Tutor he would indeed be well rewarded if he could quiet Electra. He starts to leave, but she takes him into the palace, both to reward him and honor the friend who sent him.

Comment

To Clytemnestra, the entrance of the Tutor seems an answer to her prayer. The audience, aware of the **irony** of the scene, learns the extent of Clytemnestra's fear and hatred of Orestes.

Electra calls the Chorus' attention to Clytemnestra's reaction to the news of her son's death, and laments with them (kommos) the slavery she must endure the rest of her life. Orestes has died a painful death in a foreign land, alone, without his sister's lamentations.

Chrysothemis enters, bursting with excitement. At the tomb of Agamemnon she found signs of a recent sacrifice; there were garlands and a lock of hair on the altar. Who could have shown such respect but Orestes? Surely he has returned! Electra scornfully says her hope is a dream because a witness to Orestes' death is now in the palace. Someone must have made the offering in Orestes' memory. Chrysothemis is crushed. Electra asks her if she is now willing to help end their troubles, and Chrysothemis says she is. Electra proposes that the two of them kill Aegisthus. She argues that Chrysothemis can never expect Aegisthus to permit her marriage, thereby taking the chance of her child avenging Agamemnon. What fame will be theirs if they succeed!

Chrysothemis replies prudently: she argues that two weak women can hardly expect to succeed in killing a man as strong as Aegisthus. Electra expected as much, and says that prudence is praiseworthy, but cowardice is despicable.

She tells Chrysothemis to go tell the plan to their mother. Chrysothemis goes into the palace, after saying that when Electra tries to kill Aegisthus she'll wish she had listened to the voice of wisdom.

Comment

The situation between Electra and Chrysothemis is similar to that between Antigone and Ismene in *Antigone*. The contrast between the two sisters is exaggerated in the Electra by dress and appearance. Both Ismene and Chrysothemis plead they are subject to superior force, and both are told to betray secret plans. Chrysothemis, however, is brought to the point of throwing away Clytemnestra's sacrifice and substituting one from Electra and herself.

The whole of this second **episode** is ironical (impatiently awaiting the recognition scene between Orestes and Electra, one is even tempted to call it unnecessary). It serves the enormously effective dramatic end of showing Electra and Clytemnestra under the most extreme circumstance - the death of Orestes - and their characters are tellingly revealed. The audience now knows that Clytemnestra is monstrously evil and Electra absolutely determined. (This characterization has a modern version in the opera Elektra of Richard Strauss.)

Second Stasimon: The Chorus say that even the birds are mindful of those who give them life, and that humans should behave like them. They hope Agamemnon will hear in Hades of the strife between his daughters. Only Electra is noble enough to bewail his murder. She is ready to die and the Chorus praise her as the best of daughters. They hope she will soon be raised above her foes.

Third Episode: Orestes and Pylades enter, saying they have come from Phocis with the ashes of Orestes. Electra begs for the urn and, holding it in her hands, laments having tried to save Orestes from death years before, only to have him die in a strange land. Now their foes exult over his death, and she might as well join Orestes in the grave.

Comment

This lament of Electra shows a side of her character different from the strong, hating, vengeful woman of the previous acts. Her desire for affection and her love for her brother are revealed. Thoughts of murder are forgotten as she longs to be with Orestes in death.

Orestes, moved by her lament, realizes that she has suffered far more than he. After making certain that the Chorus can be trusted, he shows her a signet ring and reveals his identity.

Comment

Of the three Electras which have survived, the recognition scene is simplest in Sophocles' play. Aeschylus uses many "clues." These are ridiculed by Euripides, who uses a scar.

Electra can scarcely contain her joy; Orestes warns her to be quiet lest someone in the house hear her and spoil his plans. He adds that time is precious and that he can hear the details of her sufferings later. Now he must know whether it is safe to enter the house or remain in ambush - and he warns Electra to keep her joy from her face.

The Tutor comes out and tells them they have been making so much noise that their plans would be known in the house if he had not been guarding the door. He tells them to hurry inside so they can make an end of their business. Electra wants to know who the Tutor is, and is told that he is the man to whom she gave Orestes as a child. Her effusive thanks are cut short by the Tutor, who again urges them to act while Clytemnestra is alone in the house. Pylades, Orestes, and the Tutor go into the house. Electra prays to Apollo to aid them in their effort to punish the impiety of Clytemnestra, then goes inside herself.

Comment

Electra's expressions of joy have sometimes been criticized as too long, but they make the necessary point that her passionate nature can find expression in joy as well as in sadness. This scene also provides the only relief from the intensity of the preceding and following scenes.

Third Stasimon: The Chorus say that the god of War, Ares, has come to bring vengeance. Orestes is the champion of the avenging Furies.

Exodos: Electra comes out of the house to warn her brother if Aegisthus should arrive. A cry is heard from Clytemnestra, calling for Aegisthus. She begs for pity, and Electra, outside, answers that she had none for Agamemnon. When Clytemnestra cries that she has been struck, Electra calls for them to strike her again.

Orestes and Pylades come out of the palace and tell Electra that Clytemnestra is dead. The Chorus warn them that Aegisthus is approaching and they go back inside.

Aegisthus enters, looking for the strangers who brought news of Orestes' death. Electra tells him that the body of Orestes is inside, and Aegisthus orders the doors thrown open so that anyone who anticipates the return of Orestes can give up their empty hopes and submit to him, Aegisthus.

The doors are opened, disclosing a shrouded corpse. Orestes invites Aegisthus to turn back the cloth from the face - and he sees Clytemnestra. Aegisthus realizes he has been tricked and wants to speak, but Electra urges them to kill him without a hearing, and throw his body to the dogs. Orestes drives him into the house, to kill him on the same spot that he killed Agamemnon. The Chorus, singing, say that the house of Atreus has passed through many sufferings and has now come to freedom.

Comment

In the versions of Aeschylus and Euripides, Clytemnestra dies after Aegisthus, at the climactic moment of the play. But these versions also emphasize Orestes' matricide, to be punished by the avenging Furies. Sophocles ends on a note of finality, stating that the house of Atreus is now purged of its curse.

When Aegisthus finally enters, he does not appear as the kind of stranger Eurydice does in the end of *Antigone*. Throughout the play his power was repeatedly referred to, and his presence seemed near. He was the most dangerous enemy of Orestes and Electra, and only the chance of his absence made their revenge possible.

THE PLAYS OF SOPHOCLES

Mourning Becomes Electra: Eugene O'Neill borrowed from both Aeschylus and Sophocles for his trilogy, *Mourning Becomes Electra*. From Aeschylus' *Agamemnon* and Eumenides the first and third parts are taken (*Homecoming and The Haunted*); from Sophocles' *Electra* the middle part is adapted (*The Hunted*). The ancient version is concerned with the return of Agamemnon from the Trojan wars to his unfaithful wife Clytemnestra and her lover Aegisthus. Grief-stricken over the sacrifice of their youngest daughter Iphigenia, Clytemnestra has sworn to avenge the girl's death by punishing her husband who made the sacrifice to propitiate the gods for a fair wind at the start of the Trojan wars. Doubly enraged by Agamemnon's return from battle with his concubine Cassandra, Clytemnestra murders Agamemnon upon his jubilant return. Two other children of this marriage, Electra and Orestes, outraged over the killing of their father coupled with their mother's open liaison with Aegisthus, pledge themselves to avenge their father's death. Electra, motivated by an intensive love for her father, persuades her brother to kill Clytemnestra and Aegisthus on the basis of Orestes' sense of justice and family honor. When the murders have been committed, Orestes is overcome by a sense of guilt and is pursued from country to country by the Furies. At last Orestes finds peace and forgiveness at the Temple of Apollo at Delphi and the Furies are changed by Pallas Athena into the Eumenides who no longer will punish matricides but will protect the city of Athens. Such then is the ancient version of matricide and revenge, known in its entirety as the Oresteia.

O'Neill's trilogy much resembles the Oresteia in plot and **theme**, for it, too, is concerned with the return of a war hero to his unfaithful wife who murders him and the revenge wrought on the mother and her lover by the daughter and son. O'Neill's play takes place at the end of the Civil War and concerns itself with a New England family of high position. O'Neill, however, utilizes

Freudian psychology as a framework, whereas Aeschylus and Sophocles employed Greek religion. Some other differences are the omission of the brother's male accomplice, such as Pylades in Sophocles' play, as well as a second sister, Chrysothemis, whom the ancient writer also added. However, like the older tragedy, the modern play is about a family of high position, the Mannons, who are cursed with tragic secrets as was the family of Agamemnon, the house of Atreus.

Here we are concerned primarily with the comparison of the second play in O'Neill's trilogy, *The Hunted*, and Sophocles' *Electra*. There are many similarities between the original title character and Lavinia Mannon. O'Neill's heroine, like Sophocles', has long mourned her father, sworn revenge on the mother and her lover, and has remained in relative isolation. Both Clytemnestra and Christine Mannon celebrate the day they killed their husbands. O'Neill's murderess, however, has planned her husband's murder more clandestinely, and lives in constant fear of its discovery. She knows that her daughter is aware of the deed and has proof which will expose her guilt and hold her up to public shame. This is not her main concern, however; what Christine Mannon fears most is that harm will come to her lover Adam Brant, who like Aegisthus is an exiled relative of the Mannons. Moreover, Christine and her son Orin have a suggestively close relationship which Clytemnestra and Orestes never had. This is one of the most important dramatic conflicts in O'Neill's play, for Christine hopes that Orin's love for her will offset Lavinia's instigation of revenge. The two women use the young man in their conflict of family honor versus filial affection, and the tension is one of the main features of the play. In Sophocles' play, Electra and Orestes have a bond which Clytemnestra cannot hope to untie, and Orestes' revenge is founded upon family honor and pity for his sister. What O'Neill stresses throughout his entire trilogy is the unnatural love of son for mother and daughter for father which has long replaced the love of husband and wife for each other. Further, O'Neill pits mother and daughter against one another in a merciless sex battle for husband and son/brother, both of whom are the women's potentially incestuous lovers. At last, Lavinia persuades her brother to murder their mother and lover by playing upon Orin's jealous love of his mother. The deeds accomplished, the brother and sister go off on a long trip to the Orient during which Orin, like Orestes, becomes haunted by guilt for his matricide.

O'Neill's trilogy, unlike the *Oresteia*, does not end in a general amnesty granted by the gods, but in the suicide of Orin, the permanent derangement of Lavinia, and her lifelong avowal to expiate the family curse by living the rest of her life in seclusion and repentance.

It might be emphasized again that O'Neill has created his play on the basis of the ancient myths but has accentuated modern Freudian psychology. The so-called "Oedipus" and "Electra" complexes are here fully illustrated along with other psychological tendencies toward "repression," whereas in the ancient drama the unseen antagonist was fate rather than subconscious motivation.

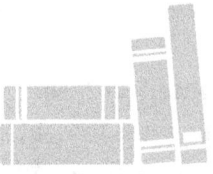

TRACHINIAE

BACKGROUND

Trachiniae is thought to have been written after Euripides' *Heracles* and to have been influenced by it. Some of its structural features are less characteristic of Sophocles than Euripides: the expository opening speech; the choral songs, which are more interludes than parts of the action; and the two-part plot. However, the cast of characters is different in each play, except for Heracles, and he has a different character. Traditionally, Heracles is represented as strong, jovial, and a great pursuer of women.

Hero-cults worshipping Heracles were widespread in the Greek world. He was highly regarded as the benefactor of man who had tamed Nature.

Zeus once visited Alcmena in the shape of her husband, Amphitryon, who was away from home. As a result of this visit she was to bear the child Heracles: thus Zeus planned to father a hero who should rule over the race of Perseus, from whom both Alcmena and Amphitryon were descended. But Zeus' wife Hera was jealous of Zeus' infidelity. She delayed the birth of Heracles and hastened the birth of Eurystheus, a grandson of Perseus by another line of descent. Thus Eurystheus was born before Heracles, and Heracles lost the birthright Zeus had intended for him. When a grown man, Heracles went mad and killed his first wife, Megara, and their children. (See Euripides, Heracles). For punishment, the Oracle at Delphi ordered him to serve Eurystheus, who assigned him the famous "Twelve Labors."

Later, he married Deianira, after rescuing her from the wooing of the river-god Achelous (see prologue, below). When he and his bride had occasion to cross the river Evenus, over which the centaur Nessus carried travelers, Nessus attempted to seduce her. She screamed, and Heracles shot him with an arrow. Before dying, the centaur gave Deianira some of the blood from the wound, saying that it would win back Heracles' love, should he ever fall in love with another woman. Later, Heracles treacherously killed a man called Iphitus, and he and his family were exiled to Trachis.

CHARACTERS

Deianira, second wife of Heracles, inadvertently kills him by using magic intended to restore his love.

Hyllus, oldest son of Heracles and Deianira.

Lichas, herald of Heracles; brings news of Heracles' triumph in Euboea.

Heracles, famous hero of the "Twelve Labors," his death is inadvertently caused by his wife, Deianira.

Old Man, looks after Heracles' welfare on journey back from Euboea.

Messenger, contradicts the lies of Lichas regarding Iole.

Chorus, maidens of Trachis.

Nurse.

Mute Characters: Iole, daughter of Eurytus, and the captive maidens from Euboea.

SUMMARY

Setting: In front of the house of Heracles, in Trachis (a city on the Euboean Gulf, in Thessaly).

Prologue: Deianira, Heracles' wife, comes out of the house with the Nurse. In a long opening speech Deianira tells the Nurse some of her past history. She begins by referring to an old saying, which maintains that a mortal's lot in life cannot be judged good or evil before he has died. Yet her own life, she says is undoubtedly sorrowful: against her will she was persistently wooed by the river-god Achelous, who appeared to her first as a bull, then as a serpent, then as a creature with the trunk of a man and the front of an ox-with water flowing from his shaggy beard. She was delivered from his frightening appearances by Heracles, who killed him. Life with Heracles has not been entirely pleasant; time after time his dangerous adventures have terrified her. She is no sooner comforted after one danger has been overcome than another appears. She is alone most of the time, and Heracles rarely sees his children.

Ever since Heracles killed the brave Iphitus, he and Deianira have lived in Trachis. For the last fifteen months, he has been away from home; she does not know where he is and has had no message. The Nurse says she has often seen Deianira weeping for Heracles, and suggests that Hyllus, her oldest son, be sent to look for him. She adds that Hyllus is approaching the house now-both advice and the man to implement it are at hand. When Hyllus enters, Deianira says he really should do something about looking for his father. Hyllus replies that if rumor is correct, Heracles was last year in Lydia, serving Queen Omphale. (Lydia-part of modern Turkey-was across the Aegean Sea from Greece.) Now he is reported to be planning, or waging, a war on Eurytus, in Euboea (a large island parallel to the east coast of Greece, across the Euboean Gulf from Trachis. Eurytus was the father of Iphitus, whom Heracles had treacherously killed). Deianira asks him whether he knows of certain oracles Heracles had left with her concerning the land of Euboea. He says he has never heard of them, and she tells him they say that when Heracles goes there, he will either meet his death or have peace the rest of his life. Hyllus, hearing this, decides to go to Euboea to help his father.

Comment

This prologue is a pseudo-dramatic dialogue: it has the form of a dialogue, but is not believable as a real conversation. The Nurse, for example, hardly needs to be told she is living in Tranchis after fifteen months there; nor is it likely Hyllus would withhold information about Heracles' whereabouts from Deianira for so long. It is conventional to say that this is a "Euripidean" prologue, but this explains neither its awkwardness nor why Sophocles should decide to imitate Euripides. Kitto, in his Greek Tragedy, cogently points out that the prologue here is not an "imitation," but a necessary device Sophocles uses to give the audience certain information relevant to his study of Heracles. This play, Kitto says, is a different kind of play from *Oedipus the King*, which worked out the tragedy of Oedipus' hamartia (error). In *Trachiniae*, several situations created by an unusual individual, Heracles, are studied, and those relevant to the action, but not part of it, are simply reported, both in the prologue and in the exodos. In *Oedipus*, past information was part of the action and was revealed when appropriate. The same technique is used in *Trachiniae* when possible, as with the Nessus **episode**, an event from the past not referred to in the prologue, but important to the action and related at the appropriate time.

Parodos: (After Hyllus departs, the Chorus of Trachinian maidens enter. They are friends of Deianira).

The Chorus pray to Apollo, asking that he tell where Heracles is because they have heard that Deianira is lonesome and unhappy, longing for him to return. Just as wave after wave is driven by the wind, so Heracles' life is a succession of troubles and honors. They tell Deianira she should not fret: Zeus has ordained that joy and sorrow should alternate in the lives of mortals, and Zeus does not forget his children.

First **Episode**: Deianira says that it is all very well for the girls of the Chorus to console her, but they have never been married, never know what it is to spend the night worrying about husband and children. Furthermore, she says, this absence of Heracles is different from his earlier ordeals; before departing this time he left like a doomed man, dividing his property among his wife and children, and saying that fifteen months later he would either die or return to lead an untroubled life.

> Comment

The prophecy regarding Heracles was made by the Oracle at Dodona, dedicated to Zeus. The will of the god was declared there by the wind rustling through the tree, hence the reference in Deianira's speech to a speaking oak. This Oracle was most influential in the heroic age, being supplanted later by the Oracle at Delphi, dedicated to Apollo.

This is the second time this prophecy is referred to, thus making the point that Heracles' life is approaching a crisis.

A messenger enters with news of Heracles. Lichas, the herald of Heracles, the messenger says, has arrived in the city with a report that Heracles has had a great victory and will soon be home. Deianira wants to know why Lichas himself has not come to her, and the messenger says he can't get away from the townspeople who have surrounded him to ask questions. The messenger had run ahead to get a reward by being first with the good news. Deianira and the Chorus sing a joyful song, praising Zeus, Apollo, and Artemis. They want to dance like the joyful Bacchanals.

> Comment

Bacchanals were worshippers of Bacchus (Dionysus), god of wine. Particularly joyful, even wild, behavior was associated with his worship.

Lichas comes in, leading a group of captive girls. Heracles, he says, is in Euboea establishing altars to Zeus in fulfillment of a vow he made before the battle. However, most of the time he has been in Lydia, serving Queen Omphale, the barbarian. For this servitude he blamed Eurytus, and Lichas tells why: Heracles and Eurytus had once been friends. Heracles visited his house once, and Eurytus taunted him by saying his sons were better archers than Heracles. He called Heracles a slave, and threw him out of the house during a banquet. Later, Heracles come across Eurytus' son Iphitus on a hill searching for some lost horses. When Iphitus was not looking, Heracles threw him off a cliff. This was Heracles' only act of treachery, and Zeus punished him because he did not seek his revenge openly. The punishment was to serve Omphale, and during his servitude Heracles vowed to enslave Eurytus and his family someday. The men of the city are now dead, and the pick of the women have been brought to serve Deianira.

Deianira says she cannot help but feel some misgivings for Heracles' triumph because his fortune may now be reversed. She pities the captive girls. She tries to speak to Iole, Eurytus' daughter, who seems to suffer more than the others. Iole will not speak, and Lichas says that she has not spoken since leaving her home. Deianira expresses her sympathy for what Iole has suffered, and she asks them all to come into the house, where she will make preparations.

Deianira starts into the house with Lichas and the captives, but the messenger detains her. He says that Lichas has lied; Heracles actually attacked Eurytus' city because he was in love with Iole. Her father wouldn't give her to him, and Lichas' story only repeats Heracles' pretext for the attack on Eurytus' city. No, the messenger says, Iole is no slave. And what is more, the whole town knows it because Lichas told the truth in his public account of events. Deianira is hurt and bewildered. The Chorus advise her to question Lichas.

About to rejoin Heracles, Lichas comes out and asks if Deianira has any message to send. She tries to question him, but he evades answering. The messenger further reminds him he is talking to his queen and questions him further, but Lichas denies the whole story. Deianira then tries another tactic, saying the god of Love is too powerful to fight against; she will never blame Heracles. Lichas should tell the truth: lying is dishonorable, and if he doesn't tell her, others will. Besides, isn't she accustomed to Heracles' other women by now? None of them has ever had harsh words from Deianira - no will Iole. Because Lichas believes that she will make allowances for Heracles' weakness, he admits the truth of the messenger's story. Lichas adds that he only lied to protect her feelings, not because Heracles had told him to. Promising that she is not going to fight Heracles' love for Iole, she takes Lichas and the messenger into the house to give them messages for Heracles and gifts in return for the women he has sent.

Comment

As the audience knows, Deianira has no intention of allowing the course of Heracles' new love to run smoothly. Therefore, her saying that the god of Love is very powerful strikes an ominous-note - is she proposing battle with the gods? (Of course she has no idea of murdering Iole either; Deianira is not a Medea or a Clytemnestra.)

First Stasimon: The Chorus sing of the power of Aphrodite, goddess of Love. Didn't the mighty river-god Achelous and Heracles, a son of Zeus, engage in combat to the death over Deianira? She sat on a hill to watch and await the victor, who would become her husband.

Second **Episode**: Deianira comes out to confide her troubles and her plans to the Chorus. Having cared for Heracles' house alone for so long, Deianira is outraged that Heracles expects her to share him with another woman. She realizes the bloom of her own youth is fading, while that of Iole is only beginning, and she is afraid of becoming a wife in name only. She tells them she is going to use Nessus' remedy: Nessus carried travelers across the river Evenus, and when carrying Deianira, attempted to seduce her. She screamed, and Heracles shot him. Before dying, Nessus told her to gather the blood clotted around his wound-it would be a charm to keep Heracles from loving any woman more than her. Now she intends to use this charm, and has, following Nessus' instructions, anointed a robe she is sending Heracles. She is, however, apprehensive about using magic, and asks the girls of the Chorus whether or not they think she is acting rashly. They say that if the magic works, she is not making a mistake - and the only way to find out is to try it.

Comment

Deianira's use of magic is not entirely innocent. Magic and witchcraft, though not uncommon, were recognized to be dangerous, and were publicly condemned. It is clear from her anxiety that she considers it somewhat disgraceful, but she intends no evil.

Lichas comes out and she gives him a box with the robe in it, saying that Heracles is to be the first to wear it and that it should not be worn in the light of the sun or the hearth, until he steps forward to sacrifice at the altar. She also reminds him to tell Heracles how kindly she welcomed Iole.

Second Stasimon: The Chorus joyfully anticipate the arrival of Heracles, and hope that the magic robe will restore his love for Deianira.

Third **Episode**: Deianira comes out of the house to tell the Chorus that a strange thing has happened, and she is worried about the robe she sent Heracles. Although she followed all of Nessus' instructions and kept the unguent of his blood away from the light, the piece of wool she used to spread it on the robe crumbled away when thrown outside in the sun. From the earth under it, blobs of foam appeared. She is afraid Nessus gave her the blood to kill Heracles. Wasn't the blood touched by the arrow which made the wound? And all of Heracles' arrows are poisoned! She is thoroughly frightened and decides that should her fears prove justified, she will commit suicide. The Chorus are trying to console her when Hyllus enters; he accuses Deianira of killing Heracles.

Hyllus says that after leaving home to search for Heracles, he found him at Cape Cenaeum, in Euboea, about to celebrate his victory over Eurytus. Lichas arrived, carrying Deianira's gift, which Heracles put on. When the flame blazed from the altar, the robe clung to him, and pain ran through his body. He questioned Lichas, who said he knew nothing about the poison, but Heracles seized him by one foot and threw him at a rock in the sea, where his skull was crushed. Then he cursed Deianira and his marriage to her. He then summoned Hyllus to approach, even if the robe killed him too, and to raise him up and carry him home. Suffering horribly, Heracles has been brought home in his ship, and Deianira can expect to see him soon, in pain, or recently dead. Hyllus hopes avenging Justice will visit Deianira and punish her. Silently, she starts for the house, and the leader of the Chorus urges her to speak and defend herself, but she goes in without saying anything.

Comment

As the play progresses, the character of Heracles, as Sophocles sees him, becomes clearer. His ordering Hyllus to approach him, even though he too might be killed by the poisoned robe, reflects the same kind of thoughtless selfishness he exhibited when he sent Iole to his home-apparently not caring whether Deianira knew the truth or not.

Third Stasimon: The maidens of the Chorus sing of the sudden fulfillment of an old prophecy which said that Heracles' servitude would end after twelve years. Does not death end servitude? The unfortunate Deianira did not foresee this; her only worry was the loss of Heracles' love. She is probably inside lamenting that she was the inadvertent cause of his death. The Chorus too lament Heracles' suffering; they place the blame on Aphrodite, goddess of love.

Fourth **Episode**: A cry of anguish is heard from inside the house: the Nurse comes out and tells the Chorus that Deianira has committed suicide. They say that the first-born of Iole is a disaster for the house of Heracles. Prodded by questions, the Nurse tells the details of Deianira's suicide. When Deianira went into the house, she saw Hyllus preparing a stretcher to carry his father on, and she ran to hide herself. Then she went to the altar and bewailed her misery. In Heracles' room, she spread coverings on his bed, said farewell to her bridal chamber, and drove a sword into her side. Hyllus, who then learned from the servants the intent of his mother in sending the robe, knelt beside her, lamenting his own slanders against her and his loss of both father and mother.

Fourth Stasimon: The Chorus wonder which woe to lament first: the death of Deianira or that of Heracles. They wish some wind would carry them away so they would not have to look back on the suffering of Heracles.

Comment

Some critics of this play have maintained that Sophocles is more concerned with the specific, individual story of Heracles than with Heracles as representative of the general human situation. The choral odes confirm this reading, being restricted mainly to comment on the immediate situation. Heracles, these critics feel, is less like most men than, say, Oedipus.

Hyllus and an Old Man who has been caring for Heracles enter, followed by attendants carrying Heracles. The Old Man urges Hyllus to speak softly, lest Heracles awake and go into his painful frenzy. Heracles, however, awakens, and he invokes Zeus to behold his suffering. This, he says, is his reward from the Greeks for ridding the world of monsters which had made it unsafe for men. He begs his son to kill him and release him from pain. This torture, given him by the fair and false Deianira, is greater than any suffering he knew from the tasks assigned him by Zeus or Eurystheus. Neither Monsters nor warriors had been able to destroy him - now it has been done by a weak woman, and without the use of a sword! He asks Hyllus to bring in Deianira so he can see whether Hyllus suffers more for his father's pain, or that of his mother when Heracles punishes her. Then the world will know that in his death, as in his life, Heracles chastised the wicked. When Hyllus tells him she is dead, and that what is causing Heracles' pain was given to Deianira by Nessus, Heracles realizes that he indeed will die. He tells his son that Zeus had once prophesied that Heracles would be killed by no living being, but by one in Hades. So it has turned out, for Nessus is dead. The other prophecy, that he would find release from bondage after Euboea, referred only to his death, Heracles adds.

Taking Hyllus' hand, Heracles has him swear to perform certain tasks: he is to carry Heracles to the top of Mount Oeta, build a large pyre, and burn him alive to end his suffering. Hyllus refuses, saying he could never be his father's murderer. He does, however, swear to do all except actually light the fire. Heracles also requests Hyllus to marry Iole because he does not want any other man to have his mistress. Hyllus is reluctant because he holds Iole responsible for Deianira's death. He only consents after Heracles threatens him with curses and makes it an explicit command. Heracles then orders that he be carried to Mount Oeta. He is lifted up and they proceed off the stage, Hyllus asking forgiveness from the gods for what he is about to do. He says that no man can see the future, but that the present is filled with suffering. All is the doing of Zeus.

Comment

The **theme** of this play has sometimes been seen as the destructive power of love, but this is not mentioned by the Chorus in the latter part of the play. Nor does Heracles mention love as the cause of his undoing. He is angry at the indignity of being killed by a woman, but the identity of the woman appears not to matter. Hyllus sees Iole as responsible, but Heracles ignores this point entirely.

It would perhaps be closer to the spirit of the play to say that the **theme** is the **irony** of fate: that it is ironical for the benefactor Heracles to suffer so greatly at the end of his life, and that Zeus should allow this to happen.

More important than abstract themes, of course, is the tragic representation of Deianira and Heracles, individuals with good intentions and high aspirations who suffer undeservedly. That the death of Deianira should be ignored by her husband is part of her tragedy; that Heracles' wife should have loved him in a way he could never understand is part of his tragedy. In the Medea, a comparable situation ends differently because the people are different.

The exodus explains the circumstances of Heracles' death and the marriage of Hyllus to Iole. Mount Oeta, where Heracles is burned, later had great importance in the cult worshipping him.

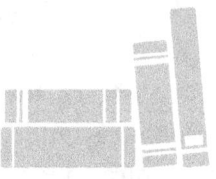

PHILOCTETES

| BACKGROUND

Presented at the tragic contest in the spring of 409 B.C., *Philoctetes* was awarded first prize. Both Aeschylus and Euripides wrote plays on the same subject which have not survived, but which were discussed in considerable detail, and in relation to Sophocles' play, by the ancient rhetorician, Dio Chrysostomus.

Heracles, suffering great pain, ordered his son to burn him alive on a large pyre. His son, Hyllus, prepared the pyre but refused to light it (see Sophocles' *Trachiniae*). This service was performed by Philoctetes, who was given in return Heracles' famed bow and its poisoned arrows, with which Heracles had once taken Troy. Years later, Philoctetes joined the Greek forces sailing against Troy. On the way, the ships stopped at the island of Chryse, where Philoctetes was bitten on the foot by a snake (see "exodos," below). The wound failed to heal and produced so foul an door that on the advice of Odysseus, the Atridae (sons of Artreus-Agamemnon and Menelaus) left him on the uninhabited island of Lemnos. In the tenth year of the Trojan War, the Greeks wanted Philoctetes to rejoin them, for an oracle had prophesied that the Greeks could not win without (1) Neoptolemus, (2) Philoctetes, and (3) the bow and arrows of Heracles, which never miss their mark. Neoptolemus accompanied Odysseus to the island of Lemnos to get Philoctetes and the bow and arrows. (In Homer, Diomedes was sent to Lemnos; in Aeschylus, Odysseus; and in Euripides, both Diomedes and Odysseus.)

CHARACTERS

Philoctetes, possessor of the bow and arrows of Heracles; suffering alone from a painful wound on the island of Lemnos.

Odysseus, one of the Greek leaders in Trojan War; comes to Lemnos to get Philoctetes and the bow and arrows of Heracles.

Neoptolemus, son of Achilles.

Spy, sent by Odysseus; disguised as a merchant.

Heracles, famous hero of the "Twelve Labors." Appears as the deus ex machina.

Chorus, companions of Neoptolemus.

SUMMARY

Setting: On the coast of Lemnos, an island in the northern half of the Aegean Sea.

Prologue: Odysseus, with Neoptolemus and an attendant, enters. He says they must not linger; Philoctetes might see them and suspect their trick to get him to Troy. Odysseus does not remember exactly where Philoctetes' cave is and asks Neoptolemus to look around for a cave entrance with a stream nearby. Neoptolemus finds it, and looks inside. No one is there, but there are a few signs of human habitation: a bed of leaves, a rudely carved bowl, a few sticks of fuel, and some scraps of cloth for Philoctetes' wound. He can't be far away, Odysseus says, because his wound makes movement too painful. He sends the attendant to stand as lookout because, he says, no man would be less welcome to Philoctetes than Odysseus. After the attendant leaves Neoptolemus says that Odysseus should tell him now whatever he has to say about their mission. Somewhat indirectly, Odysseus replies that they cannot rely on their strength or courage for success; everything depends on manner. Therefore, Neoptolemus should remember that, if Odysseus' plan seems strange or even repugnant, Neoptolemus' duty is to obey. Neoptolemus makes no promises, but asks what the plan is.

Philoctetes must be deceived, Odysseus says, and Neoptolemus must deceive him. Neoptolemus is only to reveal his own name and the fact that he is Achilles' son. His story is to be that he was wronged by the Greek leaders when they gave his father's splendid armor to Odysseus. He can malign Odysseus as much as he chooses because it will be in a good cause. Since Neoptolemus was not with the Greeks when the war began, Philoctetes will bear no grudge against him, but if he learns that Odysseus is with him, all is lost. Odysseus says that although deceit will go against the nature of Neoptolemus, the situation demands boldness - they can be just later. A Greek victory over Troy depends on getting Heracles' arms. To be deceitful for only part of a day will ensure Neoptolemus' fame. Neoptolemus refuses to descend to fraud. He, like his father, will try anything in open combat, but not flattery or betrayal. Why, he asks, don't they

> simply attack? Isn't Philoctetes lame and weak? He prefers to fall virtuously rather than achieve victory stealthily.

Comment

This play begins in a "typical" Sophoclean manner, with natural dialogue, and a natural situation; there is no expository prologue or artificial conversation intended only to give information. Information about the past relevant to the action is revealed as the play proceeds. One reason is the nature of the play rather than dedication to a particular technique. For example, to understand Neoptolemus' behavior, we should know he was brought to Lemnos before learning deceit would be necessary; therefore, we hear the past in Odysseus' version. Later, we hear Philoctetes' story - also heard for the first time by Neoptolemus - and we can compare the two stories and their effects on Neoptolemus.

Odysseus praises the nobility of Neoptolemus' attitude, and says that he too relied on strength when young; he has since learned that the soft enchanting tongue is more powerful. Neoptolemus suggests they use persuasion, but Odysseus says that Philoctetes wouldn't listen. Force would be more foolish because of the arrows. Neoptolemus is ashamed to be known as a liar, but Odysseus justifies lies which promote success. Neoptolemus says he doesn't care whether Philoctetes comes to Troy or not-didn't Odysseus tell him that he, Neoptolemus, was destined to destroy Troy? Odysseus then says that both Neoptolemus and the arrows are necessary-one or the other alone cannot succeed.

> Comment

The cleverness of Odysseus is apparent not only in his scheme for deceiving Philoctetes, but in the way he handles Neoptolemus, who knows only what Odysseus chooses to tell him about the situation. Odysseus does not reveal any more than is necessary, and that only when it will be most effective. Revealing the past only when it is relevant or necessary also increases the play's suspense. The same technique is most notably used in *Oedipus the King*. (See also the previous comment, above.)

Realizing that his own hopes for fame and honor in the Trojan War will be nullified without the weapons of Heracles, Neoptolemus agrees. Odysseus assures him that he will be praised for both bravery and wisdom. Having won over Neoptolemus, Odysseus prepares to leave lest his presence be discovered by Philoctetes. He says he will send a spy should Neoptolemus be gone long. As Odysseus leaves, he prays for success to Athena and the deceitful Hermes.

> Comment

In addition to his role as messenger of the gods, Hermes was also the god of eloquence and cunning, and, by extension of these, of fraud, perjury, and theft.

Parodos: The Chorus, companions of Odysseus and Neoptolemus, enter. Believing that Philoctetes will be suspicious of them, they ask how they should act, and declare their loyalty to their royal lord, Neoptolemus. In a lyrical interchange with Neoptolemus, they learn the lay of the land and sing sympathetically of their pity for Philoctetes' pain and loneliness. Neoptolemus says that, in his opinion, the gods must assent to Philoctetes' suffering because they do not want Troy to fall under his arrows before the appointed time. The Chorus warn Neoptolemus; they have heard a noise. It is the groaning of Philoctetes as he slowly comes toward his cave.

Comment

Sophocles has greatly reduced the portion of the play usually assigned to the Chorus. They are almost completely integrated into the action of the play, becoming a kind of minor character. With the exception of the first stasimon, there are no formal choral odes in the play. The parodos and the other stasima are choral lyrics combined in a lyric dialogue with one of the actors (epirrhematic construction).

The attitude of the Chorus is not entirely consistent. Although they express great sympathy for Philoctetes' suffering in the parodos-a sentiment not mentioned by Odysseus - they urge Neoptolemus to the base course of action. In the remainder of the play their attitude varies less than Neoptolemus', thus serving as a contrast to his extremes of attitude.

Although Neoptolemus is acknowledged to be a great warrior, he is young and inexperienced. Not only Odysseus, but the Chorus and Philoctetes address him as "my son." His moral attitude is not the stupid simplicity of a brute - he is skillful in deception when he undertakes it - but the youthful idealism to be expected from a son of Achilles, the man of action who despised deceit.

First **Episode**: Philoctetes enters, clad in rags and moving with difficulty. He welcomes Neoptolemus and the Chorus, asking that they not look on him with horror. Happy to see

Greeks, he asks who they are and how they happen to be there. Neoptolemus pretends never to have heard of Philoctetes. Philoctetes says he must indeed be hateful to the gods if such suffering as his remains unknown; surely the Greek leaders have concealed his story. He tells Neoptolemus his name and that he is the owner of the famous arrows of Heracles; he was inhumanly abandoned by Agamemnon, Menelaus, and the vile Odysseus after falling asleep on the island of Lemnos. He awoke to find the fleet gone, no companion left to help him. His bow and arrow have enabled him to keep alive on a desolate and uninhabited island. A few ships have been driven to the island by storm, and left a little food and clothing, but all have refused to carry him home.

Comment

As a matter of fact, the island of Lemnos was large, endowed with excellent ports, and inhabited. This degree of poetic license is less troublesome in the play itself than the Chorus in versions by Aeschylus and Euripides: Lemnians who improbably ignored Philoctetes' plight for years.

Neoptolemus says that he too has been ill-used by the Greek leaders. After his father, Achilles, was killed, Odysseus came to Neoptolemus, who was still at home, and said that Troy would only fall to him. He went to Troy and was enthusiastically cheered as a new Achilles. When he asked for Achilles' famous armor, however, they told him it had been given to Odysseus. Odysseus said he deserved it because he had protected both the armor and Achilles. Stung by Odysseus' proud words, Neoptolemus says he then left Troy, blaming Agamemnon and Menelaus, the Greek leaders, even more than Odysseus. The Chorus, confirming the story, sing to Earth, the mother of Zeus, of their sorrow when

Achilles' armor went to Odysseus. Philoctetes says that nothing good or just can be expected from Odysseus. He asks about Greeks he had known-Ajax, Antilochus, Patroclus - and learns they have been killed. When he learns that such scoundrels as Odysseus and Thersites still live, he bitterly concludes that the gods preserve the evil and do not deserve to be worshipped.

Neoptolemus agrees, saying that because he does not wish to live among men he cannot love, he has left Troy and will continue his journey with the first favorable wind. Philoctetes, alarmed at the news of Neoptolemus' imminent departure, begs to be taken with him. His home is only a day's journey, and all other passing ships have refused him passage. The Chorus add their pleas to Philoctetes', urging Neoptolemus both to annoy the Greek leaders and to please the gods by taking Philoctetes home. Neoptolemus warns them that they might regret their generosity, once Philoctetes is on the ship and they are close to the powerful stench from his wound. They say that they will never be reproached for that, and Neoptolemus agrees to take him. Philoctetes is overjoyed and says that he'll be ready after one last look at his cave, of which he has become fond with time. His departure is delayed by the entrance of a stranger who is Odysseus' spy (Odysseus in disguise?), dressed as a merchant and accompanied by one of Neoptolemus' men. He says that adverse winds drove him to Lemnos on his way from Troy. Learning that Neoptolemus was there, he has come to warn him that the Greeks are in pursuit of him and plan to take him back to Troy. Neoptolemus asks whether Odysseus is one of the Greeks pursuing him and the Spy replies that Odysseus had left with Diomedes - and breaks off. He asks Neoptolemus in a whisper who the stranger is, and when he learns it is Philoctetes, tells Neoptolemus to fly immediately. When Philoctetes asks what the whispering is about, Neoptolemus tells the Spy to speak openly, which he is afraid to do lest the Greeks learn of it and turn against the poor merchant. Assured that both Neoptolemus and Philoctetes are enemies of the Greeks, he reluctantly says that Odysseus and Diomedes have set out to get Philoctetes. Neoptolemus asks why they want to see the exile again; the Spy says that the prophet Helenus, son of King Priam of Troy, was captured by Odysseus and revealed many prophecies to the Greeks. One was that Troy would never fall to the Greeks without Philoctetes. The Spy warns them to leave Lemnos quickly, and hurries back to his ship.

Comment

This scene with the Spy has sometimes been considered irrelevant to the plot, but it prepares Philoctetes for Odysseus' development of the intrigue by having both Philoctetes and Neoptolemus in the same precarious position of being pursued by the Greeks, and intensifies the dependence and trust Philoctetes gives Neoptolemus. This is also the first time Philoctetes has heard the prophecy about the need for him at Troy.

Philoctetes is outraged that Odysseus thinks flattery could ever persuade him to help the Greeks. Anxious to depart, Philoctetes says he has only to get a plant that gives some relief to his wound, and his bow and arrows, which are in the cave. Neoptolemus asks that he be allowed to touch the bow, and the request is granted. He is the only person ever given that privilege; Philoctetes says he could deny nothing to Neoptolemus. They go into the cave, Neoptolemus helping Philoctetes.

First Stasimon: The Chorus sing of Philoctetes' suffering. Not since Ixion was bound to an eternally revolving wheel has anyone suffered so much. Unlike Ixion, Philoctetes did no evil, yet has been made to suffer alone on a deserted island. He has been denied the bountiful fruits of the earth; for years he has had to live on what his arrows supplied, and drink from stagnant pools for want of wine. They hope that he will now have a fairer fate with his noble friend.

Second **Episode**: Neoptolemus comes out of the cave with Philoctetes, who is carrying the bow and arrows. They are ready to go to the ship, but suddenly Philoctetes is seized with a spasm of pain. Unable to continue further, he gives the arrows to Neoptolemus to keep for him until the attack has passed. As the stabbing pain periodically wracks his body, he pleads with Neoptolemus not to leave him. He wishes such intolerable pain would fall on Odysseus and the Atridae. He begs Neoptolemus to perform for him the same service he, Philoctetes, once gave Heracles, releasing him from life and pain. His pain increases again, causing hallucinations; Neoptolemus holds him down, then releases him, and he sinks into sleep.

Comment

In a play of intrigue, suspense and uncertainty are maintained by unexpected events and the characters' moral vacilation. In *Philoctetes*, Sophocles introduces the unexpected paroxysm of pain that seizes Philoctetes, not only for surprise, but to dramatize his suffering for Neoptolemus and the audience. (Cf. a comparable device in the dramatization of Ajax's madness in Sophocles' *Ajax*.) Other surprises are the entrance of the Spy and the two sudden appearances of Odysseus.

Second Stasimon: The Chorus praise sleep as the great physician of the mind. They ask Neoptolemus what is to be done now; surely they will have no better opportunity to take the weapons. Neoptolemus says that taking the bow and arrows without Philoctetes himself would serve no purpose, and, in addition, he has given his word to stay with Philoctetes. The Chorus suggest that they carry Philoctetes to the ship; he could not resist and the wind is fair.

Third **Episode**: Philoctetes wakes up; he praises the nobility of Neoptolemus for having stayed by him despite the stench. He feels better and asks Neoptolemus to help him to the ship. Neoptolemus becomes troubled and expresses doubt about what he is doing. Philoctetes fears being left behind. Neoptolemus then blurts out the truth-Philoctetes is to be taken to Troy. Philoctetes asks for his bow and arrows back, but Neoptolemus refuses. Justice and the common cause, Neoptolemus says, demand that he obey the orders of the Atridae.

Philoctetes calls him an infamous betrayer for stealing the weapons that keep him alive. He asks the world to behold the perjury of Achilles' son, who promised help, then stole his weapons by fraud. He tells Neoptolemus to return the arms, and be himself again. Receiving no answer, he imagines life without the arms: unable even to hunt, he will become the prey of wild animals. Philoctetes says he will withhold his curse in the hope Neoptolemus will relent. The Chorus say it is time to go; Neoptolemus must make up his mind. His pity for Philoctetes is too great; he cannot make up his mind and asks the Chorus for advice.

Suddenly Odysseus enters, calls Neoptolemus a traitor, and demands the bow and arrows. He says that unless Philoctetes comes willingly, the men will carry him away by force. Philoctetes replies that before he will be taken to Troy he will kill himself; to prevent this, Odysseus orders the men to seize him. Unable to move, Philoctetes turns on Odysseus, accusing him of corrupting the noble Neoptolemus into an instrument for fraud. Neoptolemus' repentance and confession prove he is not base; the fraud comes from Odysseus' dark soul. He recalls Odysseus' scheme to avoid going to Troy, while he, Philoctetes, willingly supplied seven ships.

Comment

Odysseus feigned madness to avoid going to Troy and disguised himself as a peasant. By the stratagem of placing his child in front of the team with which Odysseus was plowing, he was shown to be sane when he turned out of the way.

The Greeks claimed that the stench of his wound made the gods refuse their offerings. Why do they want him now? Certainly the inhumanity they once showed has not suddenly changed-some message from the gods must be behind it. Odysseus claims that he is as just as any man. He tells Philoctetes to stay if he chooses; the arrows are enough. Odysseus says that with the bow and arrows perhaps he can win the honors once reserved for Philoctetes, Philoctetes begs Neoptolemus to stay, but Odysseus orders him to go. He then begs the Chorus to stay with him, and they turn to Neoptolemus for orders. He tells them to stay until the sacrifices are over and the ships ready for departure; then he will call them.

Comment

Odysseus is lying when he says the arms alone will be enough. He is apparently hoping that the fear of being left without them and a desire for glory at Troy will lead Philoctetes to change his mind.

Third Stasimon: Philoctetes laments that he is to be left alone to die in his cave. The Chorus tell him he provoked his own fate by scorning the course of wisdom, the gods, not men, have decreed what he should do. The Chorus offer their friendship, saying they are guiltless of wishing him harm. Philoctetes says that Odysseus is now laughing at him on the shore. If only his bow and arrows could know what indignity they suffer! The Chorus argue that Odysseus was only obeying the voice of Greece by asking him to join in their common cause. Their arguments anger Philoctetes and he tells them to go away, which they start to do. Then he begs them to return. He curses both Trojans and the Greeks, and asks the Chorus for some weapon he can use to kill himself. Saying that he could never face his father in Hades after having left home to fight for the hateful Greeks, he goes into the cave.

Exodus: The Chorus are about to return to the ships when Odysseus and Neoptolemus enter. Neoptolemus' conscience has worked on him, and he intends to purge himself of having betrayed Philoctetes; he has decided to return the bow and arrows. Odysseus says the whole Greek host will attack him but Neoptolemus replies that he is not afraid of doing right. When Odysseus grasps his sword, so does Neoptolemus; Odysseus backs down, saying he's decided to tell the Greeks and let them avenge themselves. As Odysseus leaves, Neoptolemus taunts him: Odysseus will always live in safety if he always acts so wisely.

Neoptolemus calls Philoctetes from the cave and asks him again to go to Troy; he again refuses. Neoptolemus surrenders the bow and arrows. Odysseus suddenly reappears and forbids Philoctetes to take them, in the name of Greece. Philoctetes raises the bow to shoot Odysseus; Neoptolemus holds his arm, and Odysseus hastily departs. Philoctetes says the Greek leaders are all boasters when they talk and cowards in the field. Neoptolemus reminds him that, having his weapons back, he can have no complaint against the friend that returned them. Philoctetes says that Neoptolemus has indeed behaved like the son of Achilles. Neoptolemus thanks him for praising his father, but adds that he has something very important to tell him. Certain misfortunes, Neoptolemus says, mankind must bear because they are inflicted by the gods. Those who inflict voluntary misfortunes on themselves deserve neither pity nor pardon, and Philoctetes is one of these. His terrible wound was inflicted by an angry heaven; it is his punishment for rashly approaching the serpent which guarded the treasures on the island of Chryse. The only way he will ever be cured is to go to Troy willingly. There the sons of the famous doctor, Aesculapius, will heal him, and, with Neoptolemus' assistance, Troy will fall. This was foretold by Priam's son, the prophet Helenus.

Philoctetes is tempted to yield, but wonders how he can consent without shame for helping those who treated him so badly. He is surprised that Neoptolemus will fight with men who withheld his father's armor from him.

Comment

Neoptolemus' confession to Philoctetes did not include an admission of his lie about the armor.

He asks Neoptolemus to remember his oath to carry Philoctetes home, and to fulfill it. Helping betrayers can only lead to becoming vile oneself. Convinced that Philoctetes will never go to Troy, Neoptolemus agrees to take him home. He is afraid the Greeks will attack his kingdom in their anger, but Philoctetes promises to defend him with the bow and arrows of Heracles.

They are about to leave together, when Heracles appears from above. (See deus ex machina, General Introduction.)

Heracles calls to Philoctetes and says that he has come from heaven to tell him the decrees of Zeus and turn his footsteps in the right direction. Just as Heracles suffered to attain glory, so must Philoctetes -then he will be happy. He must go to Troy, where he will be cured. In battle he will kill Paris, who caused the Trojan War. The spoils he is awarded must be dedicated to Heracles as a monument to his bow and arrows. Heracles tells Neoptolemus to go to Troy too, for the city cannot be taken without both of them. He warns them to be certain they venerate the gods after the city falls. Both say that they will willingly obey. Philoctetes says farewell to the island where he has known so much unhappiness, and goes out with Neoptolemus. The Chorus pray that the voyage may be safe.

Comment

Sophocles' use of the **deus ex machina** enables the ending of the play to conform to "history." In Euripides' version, Philoctetes went to Troy after changing his mind. By showing Philoctetes as steadfast in his refusal, Sophocles makes possible Neoptolemus' sacrifice of his greatest ambition-conquering Troy. Sophocles displays his characters in an extreme situation, giving greater consistency and depth to Philoctetes' hatred, and greater nobility to Neoptolemus.

OEDIPUS AT COLONUS

BACKGROUND

Oedipus at Colonus was written when Sophocles was nearly ninety years old, produced five years after his death, and was awarded first prize. The play has often been called Sophocles' best, but its concern with contemporary Athens and its religious mysticism have discouraged modern adaptations.

The action of this play takes place after the events of *Oedipus the King* and before those of *Antigone*. At the end of *Oedipus the King*, Oedipus blinded himself and asked to be sent into exile, but Creon wanted to consult the oracle first. Apparently no oracle was consulted; Creon ruled Thebes, and Oedipus remained there. Some citizens believed Oedipus to be a pollution to the city and persuaded Creon to banish him. Oedipus' two sons, Eteocles and Polyneices, did nothing to help their father, and he felt the city, taking Antigone to care for him. The brothers became ambitious to rule Thebes themselves. Eteocles won the support of the citizens, became king, and banished his brother. Polyneices went to Argos, where he married the daughter of the king, Adrastus. As the Colonus begins, Polyneices is about to lead an Argive army against Thebes, hoping to wrest the throne from Eteocles.

CHARACTERS

Oedipus, former king of Thebes; had once unknowingly killed his father and married his mother, Jocasta; they had four children.

Antigone, daughter of Oedipus who accompanies him into exile.

Ismene, daughter of Oedipus who comes to warn him of Creon's plan.

Theseus, king of Athens who gives sanctuary to Oedipus.

Creon, became king of Thebes after Oedipus; tries to take Oedipus to Thebes.

Polyneices, older son of Oedipus (usually represented as the twin of his brother Eteocles).

Chorus, old men of Colonus.

Stranger, a man of Colonus who tells the townspeople of Odeipus' presence.

Messenger, brings the news of Oedipus' death.

SUMMARY

Setting: At a grove sacred to the Furies, in Colonus, about a mile northwest of the Acropolis in Athens. (The Furies were a divine group of hideous women who pursued murderers of blood-kin for revenge. They were feared to the extent that their name [Erinyes: Furies] was avoided and a propitiary name [Eumenides: *Kindly Ones*] substituted. There was a tradition that the behavior of these women ultimately changed to fit their propitiary name [see Aeschylus, Eumenides].)

Prologue: The blind Oedipus and his daughter Antigone, their clothes reflecting poverty and hardship, enter. He asks her to inquire where they are, and wonders who will be host to them. He desires little, he says, having learned patience, a lesson taught by suffering, by their years together, and, lastly, by a noble mind. A Stranger enters and tells them they are in a sacred place, where entrance is forbidden. It is dedicated to the Eumenides-as the local people prefer to call them, he adds.

Comment

The reluctance of the Stranger to mention the real name, Erinyes, of the Avenging Furies, is an example of the power believed to be in some sense inherent in a name. When a name represents an undesirable power, as here, a name expressing the opposite quality is used instead. (See "Setting," above.)

Oedipus declares that he will never leave this place; he will stay as a suppliant.

Comment

Because of the fear the Furies inspired, their sacred grove was shunned; it is one of the ironies of the play that Oedipus feels the grove to be his destination and the Furies his protector.

The Stranger says the area is also sacred to Poseidon, god of the sea, and to Prometheus. The local people consider the hero Colonus their founder, and have erected a statue to him in the grove. They are politically subject to Theseus, king of Athens, he explains to Oedipus.

Comment

The sea-god Poseidon was not regarded as an entirely benevolent deity by the Greeks, perhaps, being a seafaring people, because of their intimate familiarity with him. Prometheus was the benefactor of man, having given him fire and knowledge (see Aeschylus, *Prometheus Bound*).

Oedipus asks the Stranger to send a messenger to Theseus, telling him that a wanderer offers him great gain for a small service, and desires to see him. The Stranger says he will tell the people of Colonus of Oedipus' presence; they will decide whether he can stay or not.

Alone with Antigone, Oedipus addresses the Furies, hoping that they will be gracious to him. Apollo, he says, once prophesied that Oedipus would one day find a hospitable shelter in their grove, and that there he would die. His hosts would be rewarded, and those who drove him away ruined. Signs that this prophecy was fulfilled would be given in earthquake, thunder, or lightning. He prays that the Furies will show him some way to close his life. He invokes the city of Athens-Athena's city-to pity the wraith who once was Oedipus.

> Comment

Oedipus' references to benefits for Athens if he is buried there reflect the ancient idea that the graves of heroes were protective influences for the land.

Hearing the approach of the old men of the Chorus, Oedipus and Antigone withdraw, hoping to learn whether they will be friendly.

Parodos: The Chorus of the elders of Colonus enter, looking for the insolent man who entered the sacred grove. He must be a wanderer, they say, for the citizens of Colonus avoid the spot, avert their eyes when they pass, and even say their prayers silently.

Oedipus enters, asking them not to regard him as a sinner. They pity his blindness, but they say he has gone too far-he must leave the forbidden ground before they will talk with him. On the advice of Antigone he comes out of the grove. The Chorus advise him to hate and love what the citizens of Colonus do.

The Chorus ask who he is, and to their horror and disapproval, he tells them he is Oedipus. They tell him to leave the city forthwith, before some calamity falls on them. Antigone pleads with them, but though they pity Oedipus' misfortunes, they fear the judgment of the gods.

First **Episode**: Oedipus says that Athens' reputation for sheltering strangers, then, is only idle praise. How can they send away Oedipus, whose acts have been only to suffer, not to do? His nature is not evil-all his acts done in full knowledge were to correct wrongs. The Leader of the Chorus says that his arguments are powerful; it must be left to Theseus to decide the case. He is being summoned by the messenger who told the Chorus of Oedipus' arrival.

Unexpectedly, Ismene, Antigone's sister, arrives. After they have happily greeted each other, Oedipus asks her the whereabouts of his two sons. As in Egypt, Oedipus says, where the men sit home weaving and the women go out to work, so his daughters have taken care of him, bearing the burden of a man. Ismene tells him that her brothers had once believed Thebes should be ruled by Creon, sparing it the curse on Oedipus' house. Now they have become ambitious for themselves, quarreled over the throne, and the younger, Eteocles, has driven out his brother, Polyneices.

Comment

In most versions of this story, the sons of Oedipus are twins. Occasionally Eteocles is the elder. Sophocles several times in his play says Polyneices is the elder, thus giving greater weight to his claim.

After his exile, Ismene continues, Polyneices went to Argos and is now contemplating an attack on Thebes. She also tells Oedipus that an oracle has prophesied that both before Oedipus' death and after, he will be desired by his people for their own welfare. This surprises Oedipus, long a pariah shunned by everyone. Ismene says that Creon is approaching. He intends to keep Oedipus near Thebes, where he will not be free, but outside the city where his presence will not be a peril. They will even refuse his body a covering of Theban dust. Oedipus declares that he will never return to Thebes, then. Ismene says that the oracle has also foretold that one day Thebes would be defeated in a battle near his tomb if he is not buried near Thebes. He asks whether his sons know this prophecy, and she replies that they do; yet they refuse to surrender their desire to rule and recall Oedipus as their king.

May the gods keep their strife alive, Oedipus says; and may it be in his power to decide the contest. Because they did nothing to prevent Creon's banishing him, Oedipus says, may Eteocles lose the throne, and Polyneices never return to Thebes. Oedipus realizes that he had once desired banishment for himself, but there was no one to help him fulfill that desire. After a time he began to feel his wrath had been too great in punishing himself; then he was driven out unwillingly. With one word his sons could have enabled him to live on in Thebes; it was left to his daughters to feed and shelter him. He declares that his sons have bartered their father for a throne. Therefore he will be buried where his grave will benefit Athens.

The Leader of the Chorus, in view of the fact that Oedipus' presence is for the good of Athens, offers him advice. He describes in detail the way to worship the deities of the grove to atone for trespassing. In the prayer, they are to be addressed as the Kindly Ones, but the words of the prayer are to be spoken inaudibly; at the end of the sacrifice, the suppliant is to retire without looking behind him. Ismene goes out to offer the sacrifice and pray.

In a lyric interchange with the Chorus, Oedipus, at their urging, reluctantly enumerates the sorrows of his life: his marriage to his mother, his children born in incest, and his murder of his father-all, he says, done without malice.

Theseus, king of Athens, enters, saying he recognizes Oedipus by his blindness and the marks of suffering on his face. He says that he too was reared in exile and is prepared to grant whatever Oedipus requests. He is mortal himself, he concludes, and may tomorrow receive as unhappy a fate.

Comment

Theseus offers asylum to Oedipus before hearing of the reward to Athens or any arguments about Oedipus' innocence. He is confident of his own power, large-hearted, and philosophical. His character is similar to that of Odysseus in Sophocles' *Ajax*.

Oedipus says that all he requests is burial in Athens, which will ultimately be to Athens' benefit. When Theseus learns that Oedipus' sons want to bury him at home. Theseus says he should return. Oedipus is unwilling because his sons let him be exiled when he wanted to stay. Oedipus explains that now they want him because the oracle has prophesied that Thebes will one day be defeated by Athens if Oedipus is buried in Athens. Theseus is surprised; Athens and Thebes are friendly to one another, he says. Oedipus tells him that only the gods are unaffected by time. Just as the body decays, so faith dies and distrust is born. Thebes and Athens will one day be enemies.

Comment

The Athenian audience would understand that Sophocles is here referring to Thebes' defeat by Athens in a battle near Colonus in 407 B.C. The first author definitely to place

THE PLAYS OF SOPHOCLES

Oedipus' death at Colonus seems to have been Euripides in his *Phoenissae*. That, and the battle at Colonus, may have led Sophocles to write this play. Colonus was also Sophocles' birthplace.

Theseus promises Oedipus whatever he wants and invites him to his house. Oedipus is afraid of those who will come for him, but Theseus assures him that nothing will happen to him that he doesn't desire.

Comment

Theseus welcomes Oedipus, and the Chorus follow his judgment. No more is heard of their disapproval or horror. They represent one level of understanding, a level limited, as it were, to fact. Theseus represents a different, and higher, level.

First Stasimon: The Chorus sing an ode in praise of Colonus and Athens, where the nightingale sings constantly in the groves, unvisited by bad weather. The Bacchanals dance happily, the crocus and narcissus bloom, and the land is blessed by the Muses and the goddess of Love. Unlike Asia or the Peloponnesus, Athens is blessed by the olive, nurturer of children, protected by Zeus. Greatest among Athens' blessings are her fine horses; before any other land, Athens learned from the gods how to tame the native rage of horses.

Comment

This famous ode, as well as other elements of the play, was probably intended to encourage the Athenians to have faith in themselves and the destiny of their city. In 405 B.C. Athens suffered a crushing defeat by the Spartans, surrendered unconditionally, and was forced to destroy the city walls. This ode is, also, one of the few nature poems in Greek.

Second **Episode**: Creon enters to plead that Oedipus return to Thebes. He says the people want him, and that Antigone deserves a better life. Oedipus, he says, should hide his shame in his own city.

Oedipus accuses Creon of betrayal and hypocrisy. Why had he not banished Oedipus when he wanted to be banished? And then cast him out when seclusion was sweet? Why try to carry him away from the one city which has welcomed him? Further, Oedipus says, Creon has no intention of taking him home-he intends to leave him just outside to frustrate the prophecy that Athens will defeat Thebes. Creon's manner quickly changes. He says he has seized Ismene as a hostage and will now take Antigone. Despite the protests of the Chorus, Creon orders his men to seize her; Oedipus blindly seeks her; the Chorus call for help. Oedipus curses Creon and his descendants with the same kind of old age he himself has suffered. Creon then states his intention of taking Oedipus too by force and goes toward him. The Chorus again call for help, and Theseus enters with his attendants. When he learns what has happened, Theseus sends soldiers to stop Creon's men at the crossroads. He says that Creon will not leave the city until Ismene and Antigone have been returned. Creon's unlawful behavior, he says, must result from a foolish old age; Thebans are in general a just people. Creon defends himself by saying that Oedipus belongs to Thebes, and that such a polluted man was by law forbidden to live in Athens.

Oedipus says his sins were all committed in ignorance: they were punishment by the gods for the sins of his ancestors. Would Creon stop to inquire of a stranger who threatened his life whether or not he was his father? In such a dangerous situation did Oedipus kill his father. Oedipus calls on the Furies to show Creon what kind of men the Athenians are. Theseus takes Creon out, ordering him to lead him to Antigone and Ismene.

Second Stasimon: The Chorus excitedly sing of their desire to be with Theseus for the battle with Creon's men. Perhaps they will fight near Eleusis, or perhaps as far away as Mount Oeta. Creon will be defeated, for Colonus has mighty warriors. They pray to Zeus and Athena for Theseus' success.

Comment

This one is a hypothetical description of an event the actors have neither time nor reason to describe in the following episode.

Third **Episode**: Theseus brings back Antigone and Ismene. Oedipus expresses his great joy, saying that in no other land has he found fairness, truth, and a fear of heaven. He wants to take the hand of Theseus, then withdraws the gesture, lest his touch pollute Theseus.

Theseus tells Oedipus that a suppliant at Poseidon's altar wants to speak to him. When Theseus says the man is from Argos, Oedipus realizes he is Polyneices, and refuses to see him. Both Theseus and Antigone prevail upon him; he can always refuse whatever Polyneices might ask. It is wrong to turn him away unheard. Oedipus has received good from others in Athens; he should be willing to bestow good himself. Oedipus reluctantly consents to see him, and requests protection from Theseus.

Third Stasimon: The Chorus sing of old age. A modest span of years is sufficient; to desire more is folly. Old age brings more grief than joy. Best is not to be born at all; having been born, the greatest good is to die. After a brief happiness of youth comes battles, and in old age, loneliness, and infirmity. Oedipus is like a northern cape in winter, lashed by wind and water.

Fourth **Episode**: Polyneices enters and laments the unhappy plight of his blind father and his exiled sisters. He upbraids himself for having done nothing to help them. Oedipus turns away from him, and he asks his sisters to plead for him. Antigone tells him to state his own case; perhaps his words will move Oedipus to reply. He says that he has been driven from Thebes even though, as the elder son, he had the greater right to the throne. Eteocles won the throne without either argument or battle but by getting the townspeople behind him. Polyneices has married the daughter of King Adrastus of Argos, and he intends to attack Thebes. He asks Oedipus for support because oracles have said that whomever Oedipus supports will win. Polyneices promises that if he becomes king, he will restore Oedipus to his own house.

Oedipus replies that he has only listened to please Theseus. Never, he says, can he forgive a son who, when he had power, drove Oedipus into exile. Polyneices will never take Thebes; both he and Eteocles will die. Oedipus curses both his sons and calls upon the Furies to drive them to Hades.

Polyneices says his preparations for the battle have gone too far to be stopped. He asks his sisters to promise that, if their father's prophecies be fulfilled and he be killed, they will give him a proper burial and funeral rites.

Comment

The subject of Sophocles' Antigone is the burial of Polyneices' body, which Creon orders exposed to the birds and dogs. Antigone defies the order.

Antigone begs Polyneices to withdraw from the battle, but he says that he could never again lead men if he backed out now. He is also humiliated at being an exile; he intends to deceive his companions by not telling them about Oedipus' prophecy. Antigone pleads with him, but he says that he will die if that is to be his fate, and departs.

The Chorus say that this has been a new misfortune for Oedipus, although it might be Fate working itself out. A roll of thunder is heard, and Oedipus sends for Theseus. He says that he is soon to die and wants to give Theseus the reward he has promised. The thunder sounds again. The Chorus pray to Zeus and call for Theseus.

Theseus enters; Oedipus tells him that he will soon, unaided, find the spot where he is to die. Its location is never to be revealed, and it will always protect Athens. Thesus will also see other mysteries in the sacred grove, and they are only to be revealed to Theseus' heir at the end of his life. Saying that he will be his daughters' guide now, he beckons to Antigone, Ismene, and Theseus. They follow him from the stage.

Fourth Stasimon: The Chorus pray to the god of the underworld that Oedipus will die without pain and pass easily to Hades. His many sufferings have earned him some assistance from the gods.

Exodos: A Messenger enters and says that Oedipus is dead. Miraculously, the blind man led them into the sacred grove. He paused at one of the branching paths and called his daughters to bring water; he washed himself and made a drink-offering. Zeus sent thunder again, and he said farewell to his daughters, reminding them that for all the suffering they have had from him, they have also had his love, which takes the pain from suffering. While they stood close to one another, there was a sudden stillness, and a voice called, saying, "Oedipus, why do you wait so long?" Oedipus called Theseus and asked him to care for his daughters. After Theseus promised, he sent his daughters away. Only Theseus remained, and when the others looked back, Oedipus had disappeared. Theseus was standing alone, shielding his eyes. Only Theseus knows how Oedipus died.

Ismene and Antigone enter, lamenting the death of their father. Antigone says he has died where he desired; now suffering is behind him. Theseus comes in, and Antigone begs him to lead them to the tomb of their father, but he refuses. Oedipus himself had ordered that the location of the tomb never be revealed lest Athens suffer. He does, however, grant Antigone's wish to go to Thebes, where she hopes to prevent the bloodshed threatening her brothers. The chorus call for an end to lamentation; all things are in the hands of the gods.

Comment

Oedipus' death represents neither approval nor disapproval of him by the gods; there is only fulfillment, in peace, of his life.

(For a different handling of a comparable dramatic situation, see Aeschylus' Eumenides.) From the audience's point of view, the personal dignity of Oedipus has increased through this play-a movement opposite to that in *Oedipus the King*.

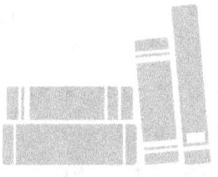

CRITICAL COMMENTARY

THE MYTH METHOD (FERGUSSON)

Francis Fergusson, an American critic and scholar who has translated Sophocles as well, has some interesting views on the Greek dramatist. He points out that the importance of the *Oedipus* play is more than dramatic or poetic, for it is upon this tragedy that Aristotle based his critical definitions, and hence upon which much subsequent literary, historical, moral, and psychological writing has been founded. Another important aspect of Fergusson's treatment of *Oedipus the King* is in the way he shows it to be a profound investigation of human experience. Around the turn of the twentieth century a group known as the "Cambridge School" began to study myth and ritual as a fundamental way of representing human experience which predates philosophy and the arts. Much of the Cambridge group's work has become incorporated into modern anthropology. It also became what is now widely used as the "myth method" of literary analysis. This method seeks to illuminate rather than to evaluate both works of art and critical theories about works of art. The premise of the "myth method" is that there are certain "archetypes" (primal patterns as named by the psychologist Carl Jung) which occur in many cultures of many ages past. These archetypes are identified with basic characters and categorized as follows; God/king/hero who is born under unusual circumstances, overcomes certain obstacles, triumphs over evil, dies or is sacrificed, and is reborn in a sacred form. The great value for Fergusson of applying the myth method to Sophocles' *Oedipus* is in the way the method shows the culmination of all the **themes** and forms inherent in the tragedy which demonstrates Sophocles' genius for the ancients as well as for us today. (See "The Myth and Ritual Pattern" in the discussion of *Oedipus the King*, above.)

PERSONAL HUMANISM AND RENUNCIATION (FALK)

Eugene Falk discriminates among personal, objective, and academic humanisms, founding his study of Sophocles' *Oedipus* and *Antigone* on the first type which obligates the critic's involvement rather than detachment, and which is based on experience rather than logic or theory. This is the framework for his thesis of renunciation as a tragic experience under certain conditions-primarily the inevitable defeat of a character's will to live by his spiritual aspirations. The process of this defeat necessarily involves suffering and distress which arouse our fear and pity (which Aristotle said were to be purged through tragedy). Falk sees renunciation as the ultimate result of the intensity of the dramatic conflict between worldliness (the will to live) and spiritual aspiration. Of *Oedipus* and *Antigone* he claims that they serve as models of dramatic intensity for subsequent plays throughout history.

In *Oedipus* it is the authentic spiritual devotion which brings about the protagonist's renunciation (of worldliness) and his self-sacrifice; in *Antigone* it is the same spiritual devotion which causes the protagonist's renunciation leading to sacrificial martyrdom. Falk contends that a character's attitude to life must be positive, for only then can the spiritual devotion bring about a genuine conflict resulting in authentic renunciation. Because the suffering of the Thebans is felt by Oedipus as his own, and because his honor dictates that he and his people are one, Sophocles demonstrates the inevitable conflict and the protagonist's self-imposed punishment. Sophocles demonstrates why Oedipus feels guilty in spite of the fact that all his misdeeds were done unwittingly. Since the innocent suffer as well as the guilty, as the plague demonstrates, the concept of Sophoclean justice is one of personal humanism - the interdependence, transference, and inheritance of guilt, or inevitable involvement. Falk's major contention is that Oedipus' search for his identity is a search for his own guilt. His decision to remain alive, although suffering mutilation and exile, meets the conflicting needs of his devotion to life and his spiritual aspirations. In this way we can estimate the scope of his heroism.

Antigone's tragic heroism is shown in contrast to the figure of Creon. Creon's fate is based on his rigidity, which leads to his inevitable doom. Antigone's is one of renunciation, and according to Falk the much greater because of it; Creon endures while Antigone exercises the self-denial and self-sacrifice of true personal humanism; that is, the tragic action is determined by her free choice and resolution. Antigone's spiritual aspirations may be seen more than as an attempt to preserve family honor by burying her brother Polyneices; where she not to bury him, it would be the disavowal of a sacred duty according to Greek religion. Thus her devotion to life is brought into conflict with her spiritual aspirations, and the result is inevitably renunciation and sacrificial martyrdom. Death is not the escape from life that it was for Jocasta, for her fear of death and desire for life are greater and she must overcome them in order to perform the sacrifice. Having sinned only against man (Creon) and not the gods, she is sinless in the larger sense. Hence her death is a measure of true heroism, and authentic tragic martyrdom.

The heroism of both Oedipus and Antigone is the result of devotion to duty, not martyr's passion. Falk sees their heroism as the most elevated kind, one which seeks to re-establish order for the good of the living, with the appropriate measure of renunciation and self-sacrifice that engenders authentic tragedy.

THE PROFUNDITY OF SOPHOCLES (KITTO)

H. D. F. Kitto reinforces the consensus of critical opinion that *Oedipus Rex* is the all-time masterpiece of dramatic construction. He praises *Electra* for its dramatic excellence as further proof of Sophocles' excellence, for that play has inherent in it all the force of rhetoric, description, incident, and character without the use of artificial devices. The action itself displays the heroic qualities of Electra. Kitto, like Fergusson, subscribes to the idea that the myth is more important than the character, and he praises Sophocles for utilizing the myth to illuminate the character of Electra. Kitto praises *Antigone* on the same grounds as *Electra* in that the heroines' personal sorrows are symbolic of greater, almost divine sorrow, and thus the characters can be seen in their largest sense. Moreover, according to this critic, Sophocles' characters are individuals yet monuments, but are not "stock characters," who are usually considered one-dimensional. As a dramatic artist, then, Kitto sees Sophocles as an unsurpassed master for his lyric poetry, economy, and presentation.

However, the critic is equally concerned with Sophocles as a profound thinker. Although many scholars and critics contend that Sophocles was orthodox in religious matters and not as original a thinker as Euripides or Aeschylus, Kitto takes the position that religion was used by Sophocles in an original fashion-as a controlling element, and that divine powers are as actively involved in the dramas as are the human.

Kitto is concerned, however with what the fundamentalist religious views in Sophocles' plays mean to the drama, not to the man. His conclusion is that Sophocles' religious orthodoxy demonstrates dramatically the interaction of human and divine powers so as to establish a philosophical relationship as a representation of the natural order of things; that the gods' action plus mortal action re-establishes after the conflicts a natural order which is both human and divine. Consequently, we perceive Sophocles' philosophy as seemingly religious orthodoxy which actually represents the organic relationship between human and divine action-universal order.

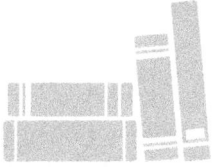

SOPHOCLES

ESSAY QUESTIONS AND ANSWERS

AJAX

Question: Discuss the functions of the following minor characters in *Ajax*: Athena, Tecmessa, the Atridae, Eurysaces.

Answer: Athena appears at the beginning of the play and says that she has caused the madness of Ajax. This madness, however, is not without other motivation; that is, it is not an arbitrary divine act. It is shown as Ajax's reaction to what he thought was the unjust award of Achilles' arms to Odysseus. His pride was offended to the point that he acted insanely. No one in the play, not even Ajax himself, believes him to be absolved of responsibility because Athena is the immediate cause of his madness. She functions therefore (as the gods do in Euripides' *Hippolytus* and, frequently, in Homer), as a symbol of a natural moral order. Ajax's pride, madness, and punishment are related to each other by Athena: the world of events is related to the moral order.

Tecmessa, Ajax's concubine, first appears in the play as a "messenger," reporting the events which occurred when Ajax arrived in his tent after slaughtering the animals. Because of her status in Ajax's retinue-she and Ajax clearly love and respect one another-her presence is well-motivated, and her reactions are more emotional than those of the conventional messenger. She can make the appeal of a wife to an audience; in fact, her lack of legal status gives the loss of her protector added pathos.

Eurysaces, the son of Tecmessa and Ajax, is used by Sophocles purely to intensify the emotional effect at the two highly dramatic moments: at the end of the scene in which Ajax realizes what he did while mad, and during the scene with Agamemnon and Odysseus. In the latter scene, the woman and child are visual presences only, presenting a pathetic tableau over the body of Ajax.

Agamemnon and Menelaus, the Atridae, represent secular authority, a force different from, but parallel to, that of Athena. The two forces are mentioned together in Ajax's speech to his followers before his suicide. There Ajax says both forces must be obeyed because they are powerful; he compares the inevitable sequence of the seasons of the year to the inevitable necessity for submission to authority. However, in the speech he makes alone before his suicide, he does not imply that those holding earthly power are necessarily in the right; he prays that Zeus will punish where he, Ajax, failed. Sophocles' view of the Atridae appears similar to that of Ajax. Both Menelaus and Agamemnon argue for obedience in the name of public order, but both are willing to sin, as Odysseus points out, to satisfy their personal cravings for revenge. The Atridae and Ajax thus function as parallel examples of error; their moral position is opposite that of Odysseus.

ANTIGONE

Question: Compare the characters of Antigone and Ismene.

Answer: As sisters of Polyneices, both Antigone and Ismene would like to see the body of their brother, Polyneices, receive proper burial. It is Antigone, however, who proposes that the decree of Creon forbidding such burial be disobeyed. In her refusal to oppose Creon, Ismene earns the epithet of "weak sister." She takes refuge in the traditional sheltered life women led in Athens, claiming that a woman cannot hope to succeed in any attempt to defy men. She is not, however, without courage. When Antigone receives the death sentence, Ismene chooses to die with her. In fact, she falsely confesses to having helped Antigone. Her weakness, therefore, is not her whole character. Emotion plays a strong role in her decisions; her reason, for example, for wanting to die with Antigone is that she could not bear to live without her.

Antigone, on the other hand, is strong-willed; she is defiant of authority to the point of stubbornness. She refuses the advice of the Chorus as adamantly as she refuses that of Ismene. Her unswerving dedication to the divine laws gives her character the intensity of a Medea or a Clytemnestra, but without their faults. Another side of Antigone is shown in her farewell speech. There the intensity for her suffering, her loneliness, and her reluctance to die show her more human, unheroic side. Her references to the fact that she must die without having been married make her pitiful. But the fact that she never wavers in her resolve shows her to be, ultimately, larger than life, a heroic woman.

Question: To what extent can Creon be considered **protagonist** of *Antigone*?

Answer: A striking feature of *Antigone* is the length of time Creon is on stage-much longer than Antigone. Also, the exodos is concerned almost exclusive with the sufferings of Creon. While such "statistical" evidence cannot by itself prove the case, it at least shows the relative extent to which Creon is directly engaging the interest of the audience. Much of the time he does not engage their sympathies, however. He is a tyrant who causes Antigone to suffer. Yet the logic of his case is seconded by the Chorus, who take the conventional view and argue in the name of prudence. Since Creon argues for the good of the state, it immediately appears that the Chorus and Creon represent a different level of morality, a different kind of philosophy from that of Antigone. Her arguments are based on personal love, religious duty, and individual obligation. The Chorus and Creon argue on the basis of public obligation and social duty; they completely ignore love between individuals. The third stasimon, for instance, describes love as madness, an undesirable visitation by Aphrodite which unseats the rational faculties of man. Since tragic personages are good men who err, according to Aristotle, Creon can be considered a tragic personage only to the extent that he can be considered a good man. The conclusion of the play shows Antigone to be right - not Creon, nor the Chorus when they sympathize with him.

OEDIPUS THE KING

Question: Compare Jocasta's moral integrity and strength of character with Creon's. Give examples from the play to support your statements.

Answer: Moral integrity implies wholeness, perfect condition, and uprightness of principles in a person. Honesty and sincerity are associated qualities. In *Oedipus the King*, Creon is represented as a man who is second to the king in position and authority. When defending himself from Oedipus' accusations that he wants the throne, he makes the point that he would have nothing to gain by wearing the crown, for people already seek his assistance to plead their cases with the king; he can now be every man's friend, not having to be responsible for decisions people might dislike. Unlike Teiresias, he does not lose his temper when Oedipus falsely accuses him, but remains moderate, reasonable, and equable. Such behavior indicates that he is at peace with himself, is confident of his rightness, and perhaps has even a certain faith that he will be vindicated before it is too late. Of course, it might merely indicate a sophistic skill in argument and great self-possession unless it were confirmed by other evidence, such as comes in the last scene. There he is clearly intended to be seen as the person in supreme control. Considering the premium placed on honor in his society and the way he was treated by Oedipus, some degree of vindictiveness might be expected and even approved of, but does not appear. Instead, the strength of character he exhibited in restraining himself reappears in the calm authority with which he concedes, even anticipates, Oedipus' desire to see his children, and then firmly denies Oedipus' wish that they accompany him in exile. His earlier avowal that he is not ambitious for power is confirmed when he delays Oedipus' exile until the gods have been consulted. His moral integrity, in short, appears to be complete and perfect.

Jocasta, on the other hand, exhibits neither high principles nor consistent principles. In her first appearance she attempts to arbitrate the quarrel between Oedipus and Creon, and, with the help of the Chorus, succeeds. Her reason for doing so, however, is not so much in the interests of truth as in the simple desire for domestic peace. (Creon, of course, is her brother, although no issue is made of that.) At the end of the same scene, she attempts to reassure Oedipus by arguing that prophecies are unreliable, that they are, in fact, lies. Her motive, again, appears to stem not so much from any strong conviction as from a desire to quiet Oedipus and make him happy. Although skeptical of oracles, her prayer to Apollo displays a conventional attitude to religion.

Her crucial scene is the one in which the messenger from Corinth appears. In it she learns the truth of her relationship to Oedipus, and before he can do the same, asks that he stop his search for his parents and his own identity. Oedipus doesn't make the connection Jocasta perceived until the herdsman comes in. Jocasta's attempt to stop his inquiry indicates, as did her attitude toward oracles, that her motives are not the result of principle. (The only principle which might be ascribed to her is that of maintaining the status quo, which is less a principle than an attitude.) There is some implication that, if Oedipus stopped the inquiry, she would keep the secret herself, but this, fairly, is only speculation. In comparison to Creon, however, Jocasta cannot be considered to have great moral integrity, nor can her strength of character be said to approach his. This is best seen in her suicide; she flees the reality of her situation shortly after learning what it is.

Question: Why does Oedipus blind himself?

Answer: The striking thing about Oedipus' blinding himself is that he could have satisfied the gods and removed the plague from Thebes "merely" by accepting banishment. The messenger reported that as he blinded himself, Oedipus had said his eyes had too long looked on the forbidden (knowing his mother as his wife), and too long failed to see what they should (his real parents). No more, he said, shall they look on the wrongs he has committed (reminders of his sin: the city, the palace, his children). When the Chorus ask him why he has blinded himself, he says only that nothing can ever appear sweet to his eyes again. Considering his passionate nature, his quick temper, and the sudden shock with which the truth came to him, some violent reaction could be expected. Banishment is no longer adequate because the crime is no longer the same - the murder of Laius is not mentioned in the exodos. Even as murder, that crime has changed from homicide to parricide. Because Oedipus was never a person to take refuge in the letter of the law, he does not do so now. As a highly principled and eminently just man, he is horrified by his own wrongs and turns against himself, literally destroying the sight which had betrayed him. As king, the exemplar of his people, he is punishing a rare and revolting crime.

Dramatically, his blinding of himself is also a symbolic act completing the implications of Teiresias' statement that the blind man sees and the seeing man is blind. It also creates a new Oedipus, his whole relationship to the world transformed, about to appear in an alien world, suffering in repentance, a victim of a fate that appears malign, but also curiously passive.

TRACHINIAE

Question: Discuss the characters of Deianira and Heracles.

Answer: Deianira has the misfortune to be the wife of the notorious pursuer of women, Heracles. The pathos of her situation results from the fact that she knows his reputation, and loves him in spite of it. Yet she is no passive sufferer, resigned to taking second place in Heracles' affections. She resorted to magic she knew to be dangerous, but from her point of view there was no alternative. To understand her character it is important to note that she never contemplates revenge, either against Heracles or against Iole. Her bitterness is reserved for the fate which keeps Heracles away from home, and the mischance which led her to accept Nessus' help at its face value. She is not, however, a perfect character. She not only resorts to magic, but she uses deceit to get the truth from Lichas. And although she knows that she would be struggling with the gods if she does not accept Heracles' unfaithfulness, she does what she can to thwart his passion.

Much of what the audience feels about Deianira results from the contrast between her character and Heracles'. She is, by comparison, unselfish, as shown by her continued sympathy for the plight of Iole. To malign Iole would show Deianira unperceptive; she knows Heracles only too well. The strongest examples of his selfishness occur when he asks Hyllus to raise him up in Euboea, and when he tells Hyllus to marry Iole. He ignores the possibility that Hyllus too might be killed if he touches the robe, even mentioning it as if he were testing Hyllus' loyalty. His reason for wanting Hyllus to marry Iole is only to keep her from any other man.

When Heracles sent Iole ahead to Trachis, he felt no shame, or even curiosity, about Deianira's feelings; he ignores Deianira's death, thinking only of his own dishonor; and he regards Iole as a piece of property-something to be kept from strangers.

On the other hand, Heracles was the greatest man in the world and he would have been stupid not to recognize it, and less than honest if he failed to admit it. His sacrifices were undoubtedly great, and his end was certainly unjustified. And as the audience knew, he would take a place among the gods and be worshipped like them.

ELECTRA

Question: Discuss the moral issues raised by *Electra* and the way they are related to the characters.

Answer: Broadly speaking, the central moral issue raised in *Electra* is that of crime and punishment. Clytemnestra has killed Agamemnon and admits it, indeed boasts of it. Her justification is that he deserved punishment for having sacrificed Iphigenia to Artemis at Aulis. Her motive is suspect, however, because she took Aegisthus as her lover several years before Agamemnon's return from the Trojan War. Agamemnon's discovery of this would have resulted in her own death or in banishment; her alternatives at the time of his return were either to leave with Aegisthus or to kill Agamemnon. In Sophocles' *Electra*, the Chorus and Electra both consider Clytemnestra to have acted from lust. Her justification, then, never strong, gains her no sympathy from anyone in the play.

The action of the play itself is concerned more with Electra and Orestes, of course, than with Clytemnestra. Orestes has instructions from the Delphic Oracle to take his revenge with his own hands; that is, he is not to arrive with an army and attack the city. The emphasis here is on the personal, rather than public, nature of the crime and its punishment. He himself is motivated not only by the spirit of Justice, but by the very human desire to come into his proper inheritance of the kingdom of Argolis and the wealth of his father.

In comparison to Electra, there is a distant, almost cold quality to the actions of Orestes. He was a child when Agamemnon was killed; he has been away for years, and the injustices of Clytemnestra and Aegisthus are for him merely something he has heard of and not experienced.

Electra, at the time of Agamemnon's murder, was old enough to realize the danger to Orestes, and to send him away. Her life has been spent publicly embarrassing Clytemnestra and Aegisthus - and suffering the consequences of their dislike. She has kept alive the memory of her father, and fed her hatred of his killers. Her desire for revenge has an intense personal quality entirely lacking in Orestes. Abstract Justice means less to Electra than the gratification of a thirst for blood growing from her hatred. The rightness of her essential attitude is confirmed by the Chorus, who throughout the play are more on her side than on Chrysothemis'. They deplore her excesses, but they absolutely disapprove of Chrysothemis' compromises; and their sympathy for Electra's cause increases as the play progresses. It is indeed in the passionate nature of Electra, rather than the flat pusillanimity of Chrysothemis, that Clytemnestra's nature is reborn. Electra's moral position stems largely from the fact that she is the immediate victim of wrongs inflicted because she will not forget the injustices of the past.

It would have improved the moral positions of Orestes and Electra if Sophocles had unequivocally stated that Apollo approved of their killing Clytemnestra. He does not, perhaps feeling that at best the desires of the gods are obscure, and that this in itself is one of man's difficulties. At the end of the play the Chorus say that the house of Atreus has now come forth in freedom, but the members of the Chorus are maidens, not gods, or even wise old men. They would naturally sympathize with the young and disinherited, and they would be pleased that they had chosen the winning side before the issue was certain. Orestes, too, after the death of Clytemnestra, said that all was well within the house if the oracle spoke well. His certainty of his rightness is qualified, not absolute. This might help explain the reason for Aegisthus' being killed last. No one doubts that his murder is justified, and thus the play ends with an act morally justifiable. Ending with the death of Clytemnestra would have left the final action matricide, about which, incidentally, very little is said in the play itself.

The play as a whole perhaps solves the moral problem of punishing Clytemnestra almost as if it were an aesthetic problem. At the beginning of the action there is an imbalance of right and wrong -Agamemnon has been killed and no one has been punished. Orestes and Electra are disinherited - and no one champions their cause. By the end of the play this imbalance has been corrected, and the rightness of the action occurs with the completeness of the action. Alone among the three Electras to have survived, Sophocles' has no sequel. Aeschylus' was the second of a trilogy, and Euripides' tells the future with the **deus ex machina**. Only Sophocles' *Orestes* ends the curse on the house of Atreus with his own hands.

PHILOCTETES

Question: Discuss Sophocles' use of contrast to illuminate character.

Answer: In *Philoctetes*, Sophocles contrasts characters with opposing temperaments, purposes, and moral standards. The resulting clashes dramatize various aspects of the personalities involved. In the prologue, for example, Neoptolemus and Odysseus are contrasted. Neoptolemus, young and idealistic, has goals in life inherited from the example of his father, Achilles. He desires to win glory by arms, in open combat. Like his father, he would approach difficulties head on, physically attacking those who oppose him and defending those who support him.

Odysseus, traditionally famous for his cunning, has this aspect of his character emphasized by Sophocles. His analysis of the situation, of course, is, ironically, correct, for Philoctetes does not give in to persuasion, and, as long as he has the bow and arrows, force would be useless. Yet however correct Odysseus is, the audience sympathizes with the viewpoint of Neoptolemus. The conflict between them, therefore, changes from a question of means to a question of ends-is the Trojan War worth winning if personal honor must be lost? Odysseus maintains that success justifies dishonor, indeed transforms it into honor.

He has on his side the compelling arguments of patriotism and duty. Neoptolemus, however, is never convinced by the appeal to his patriotism. He first gives in to Odysseus because having the arms will enable him to win personal glory. His appeal to Philoctetes, late in the play, is based not on patriotism but on the acceptance of divine order. The contrast between Neoptolemus and Odysseus emphasizes the straightforwardness of Neoptolemus and the deceitfulness of Odysseus.

The contrast between Neoptolemus and Philoctetes shows much more clearly the moral stature of Neoptolemus. Not only is he touched by Philoctetes' suffering as Odysseus never is, but he sees the justice of Philoctetes' refusal to help the Greeks. He sees this despite the extent of his own personal involvement in Philoctetes' decision. His dedication to the principles of a code upholding glory in combat as the chief end of life is jeopardized.

If he fails to get Philoctetes and the arms of Heracles, he cannot be the champion who brings victory to the Greeks. In making his decision to return the arms, he chooses a moral code based on personal relationships over one based on public necessity, and demonstrates his strength of character, his independence, and his inherent nobility. When he agrees to take Philoctetes home, he carries his defiance of the Greeks a step further by removing Philoctetes from the vulnerable cave on Lemnos. He even makes the decision before knowing Philoctetes will help him defend his kingdom.

Philoctetes is contrasted to both Odysseus and Neoptolemus. In reminding Odysseus that he had once tried to avoid going to Troy, Philoctetes effectively improves his own moral position and attacks Odysseus' arguments for patriotism. The most distinctive fact of Philoctetes' life, however, is his wound and his suffering. He has nursed his hatred for years under the most extreme conditions. While Odysseus is able to anticipate the hatred, he underestimates its intensity and its effect on Philoctetes. For Odysseus apparently believes that if he takes the weapons, Philoctetes will surrender; if not, he can be bodily carried to Troy. Before Odysseus can order him carried to the ship, however, Neoptolemus returns the weapons. Philoctetes, like Neoptolemus, chooses personal morality over public. The representatives of the public welfare, he seems to say, cannot expect their claims to override individual suffering or an individual's respect for himself.

OEDIPUS AT COLONUS

Question: Compare Sophocles' characterization of Oedipus, Antigone, and Creon in his three plays on the Theban story.

Answer: Oedipus appears in two of the plays, *Oedipus the King* and *Oedipus at Colonus*. In the first he begins as the successful and confident king, loved by his people. When the people appear to him and beg for help in ending the plague, he confidently accepts the duty, implying that one who could successfully rid the city of the Sphinx can also rid it of the plague. He prosecutes the inquiry briskly, almost ferociously when he thinks Teiresias is obstructing him by being unwilling to reveal his prophecy. When he displays his anger against both Teiresias and Creon, we see the man who killed Laius and his companions at the crossroads. Oedipus is a good man; he is also passionate and hasty. These two sides of his character combine to bring about his downfall. His lifelong desire to act immediately in the cause of good led him to renounce Corinth when he thought himself a threat to Polybus. The same instinct led to his tragic discovery of parricide and incest. At the end of *Oedipus the King*, he is a completely broken man, obsessed with punishing himself. He blinds himself and longs to be exiled as a pollution of the land.

In the Colonus, we learn that while he lived on in Thebes, he changed. He begins to consider his punishment of himself to have been excessive. The shock of discovery wearing off, he contemplates the fact that all his crimes were committed in innocence. When he is exiled, he is the victim of men consciously doing wrong for their own selfish ends. In exile, blind, and poverty-stricken, he is refused sanctuary until he comes to Athens. His humility changes in quality, no longer being the desperate shame and desire for self-punishment which he felt when he blinded himself. When he speaks to the Chorus in the Colonus, for example, he realizes he is famous as a polluted man, but he can defend himself for the innocence of his intentions, and he can offer Athens benefits in return for sanctuary. There is, in short, a degree of pride and dignity in him now that was completely absent immediately after his discovery. Theseus accepts him before hearing any justifications, seeing him as a victim of Fate, not a criminal.

The old angry Oedipus appears in the scene with Creon, and again when Polyneices appears. Oedipus is unforgiving to those who live only for themselves. To a modern audience, he appears hard, even unreasonable. Yet as Sophocles presents him, purged of ambition and near to death, he can speak with the authority of a judge. He dispenses justice to Polyneices, who remains ambitious and deceitful. He tells his daughters that their love for him has erased their suffering, freeing them from the family curse just as Theseus freed Oedipus from the horror of the Chorus-by invoking a higher morality.

Antigone hardly appears at all in *Oedipus the King*. Probably very young, she is brought out with Ismene, and Oedipus makes his farewell. She may, in later life, have had some memory of that day; if so, it is not mentioned. There was no chance, however, that she would not be told what happened. Her father is famous throughout Greece as a sinner; she learns this at firsthand when guiding him in his search for a place to die. In the Colonus she is shown as a model daughter, gentle with her father and completely dedicated to his interests, a gentleness which extends to her sister and brother. When Ismene appears, Antigone does not upbraid her for not having accompanied Oedipus in his earlier wanderings, and when Oedipus curses Polyneices, Antigone receives Polyneices' request for burial without rancor. At the end of the play her concern is with preventing bloodshed between her brothers.

In *Antigone* she is a much stronger, forceful personality, but she is still motivated by piety and consideration for others. A line of harshness does appear, however, in her impatient dismissal of Ismene and her denunciation of Creon. Her provocation, of course, is great, and there is a need for immediate action. She never, however, approaches the extreme vindictiveness and hatred of another Sophoclean heroine, Electra.

Creon appears in all three of the Theban plays, and his character is quite different in each. Being a minor character, consistency of representation is sacrificed to immediate dramatic needs. In *Oedipus the King*, the equanimity, self-possession, and patience of Creon contrast to the opposite qualities of Oedipus. At the end of the play, his sympathy and understanding are a foil to the desperation of Oedipus. He remains a minor character, however, not a model of what a good king should be.

More an example of kingship is the Creon in *Antigone*. Having the opportunity, indeed necessity, of exhibiting leadership, of acting for the interests of the state, he orders the exposure of Polyneices' body. When Antigone defies him, he responds much as might be expected from a new king whose first official decree is broken. He justifies himself by a theory of kingship which appears almost impeccable, but his specific application of the theory is at fault. When he says that even unjust laws should be obeyed he goes too far, just as he went too far when he denied religious burial to Polyneices. The Creon of *Oedipus at Colonus* is little more than a stock villain. His motives are selfish, his methods deceitful, and his resort to force unlawful. Sophocles cannot even be said to malign him, so clearly is his role subservient to the needs of the play.

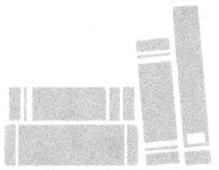

BIBLIOGRAPHY AND GUIDE TO FURTHER RESEARCH

THE FIFTH CENTURY

Agard, W. R. *The Greek Mind* (Princeton, 1957).

Bowra, C. M. *The Greek Experience* (New York, 1958). An illustrated history of ancient Greek civilization.

Cambridge Ancient History, Vol. V (Cambridge, 1935).

Hamilton, Edith. *The Greek Way to Western Civilization* (New York, 1948). Usually referred to as simply *The Greek Way*, this book has undergone three major revisions, and is a monument in the field of classical studies. It is one of the essential books for all students of Greek literature and art, yet it is neither overly specialized nor difficult, but rather an extremely readable account of the Greek influence on Western culture. The book deals with the artistic, dramatic, spiritual, religious, social, and intellectual aspects of ancient Greece and correlates each with aspects of contemporary Western civilization. It contains a chapter on Sophocles which should prove extremely valuable. (Also available in paperback.)

Kitto, H. D. F. *The Greeks* (Penguin Books, London, 1951).

BRIGHT NOTES STUDY GUIDE

MYTHOLOGY

Graves, Robert. *The Greek Myths*, 2 vols. (Penguin Books, 1955).

Harvey, Sir Paul. *The Oxford Companion to Classical Literature* (Oxford, 1937).

Blakeney, E. H., ed. *Smith's Smaller Classical Dictionary* (Everyman's Library, 1937).

GENERAL WORKS ON CLASSICAL DRAMA

Greene, Wm. Chase. *Moira: Fate, Good, and Evil in Greek Thought* (Cambridge, Mass., 1944). A detailed study of fate and fatalism in Greek literature, philosophy, and drama in historical and critical perspective.

Harsh, Philip Whaley. *A Handbook of Classical Drama* (Stanford University, 1960).

Kitto, H. D. F. *Greek Tragedy, A Literary Study* (Doubleday Anchor Books, New York, 1954).

Legrand, Philippe E. *The New Greek Comedy* (London, 1917). A tableau of Greek comedy during the period called "new" (after 330 B.C.) with historical and critical explanations.

Norwood, Gilbert. *Greek Comedy* (London, 1932). A history of Greek comedy concentrating on the schools of Crates, Eupolis, Aristophanes, and Menander. Concentrates on the meter and rhythm especially found in Greek comedy.

Prentice, William Kelly. *Those Ancient Dramas Called Tragedies* (Princeton, 1942). An explanation and analysis of Greek Tragedy with an extended contextual definition of the term "tragedy" throughout the work.

Bates, W. N. *Sophocles: Poet and Dramatist* (University of Pennsylvania Press, 1940).

Bowra, C. M. *Sophoclean Tragedy* (Oxford, 1944). Essential to the study of Sophocles, this is a work of the highest critical scholarship, yet an extremely readable and enjoyable analysis of the ideas behind Sophocles' tragedies. The author has carefully presented the critical consensus along with his own opinions.

Falk, Eugene H. *Renunciation as a Tragic Focus* (Minneapolis, 1954). This study of five plays includes essays on Sophocles' *Antigone* and *Oedipus*. The emphasis of this work is on the aspect of personal humanism as discriminated from academic or impersonal humanism which implies involvement rather than detachment. It is an interesting point of view and well worth investigating.

Fergusson, Francis. *The Idea of a Theater* (Princeton, 1949). A study of ten plays illustrative of the changing perspective of dramatic art. Excellent theoretical and analytical guide to understanding dramatic form and idea throughout a range of dramatists from Sophocles to T. S. Eliot. (Also in Anchor paperbacks.)

Kirkwood, G. M. *A Study of Sophoclean Drama* (Ithaca, 1958).

Kitto, H. D. F. *Sophocles: Dramatist and Philosopher* (London, 1958). A solid treatment of Sophocles and his work in the light of human and divine considerations. A worthwhile modern scholarly treatise.

Sheppard, J. T. *Aeschylus and Sophocles: Their Work and Influence* (in Our Debt to Greece and Rome) (Longmans, New York, 1927).

Waldock, C. H. *Sophocles the Dramatist* (Cambridge, 1951).

Webster, T. B. L. *An Introduction to Sophocles* (Oxford, 1936).

Whitman, C. H. *Sophocles; A Study of Heroic Humanism* (Cambridge, 1951).

Wilson, Edmund. *The Wound and the Bow* (New York, 1929). Seven studies in literature, the last of which is of Sophocles' *Philoctetes*. An interesting reappraisal of the play showing its relationship to other Sophoclean works and to modern psychology and philosophy.

RELATED STUDIES

Harrison, Jane. *Themis* (Cambridge, 1927). A discussion of primitive art, culture, and aesthetics. See especially Gilbert Murray's "Excursus on the Ritual Forms Preserved in Greek Tragedy," pp. 341-363. (Also in Meridian paperback).

Mullahy, Patrick. *Oedipus, Myth and Complex* (New York, 1948). A review of psychoanalytic theory based on the Oedipus trilogy.

Weisinger, Herbert. *Tragedy and the Paradox of the Fortunate Fall* (East Lansing, 1952). A "myth" interpretation of the tragic experience and reaction to it.

www.ingramcontent.com/pod-product-compliance
Lightning Source LLC
LaVergne TN
LVHW011710060526
838200LV00051B/2843